COLLECTED POEMS OF
LUCIO PICCOLO

Lucio Piccolo di Calanovella was born in Palermo on 27 October, 1901, and died 26 May, 1969. He published the following books:

Canti Barocchi E Altre Liriche
(Mondadori, Milan, 1956).
Preface by Eugenio Montale.

Gioco A Nascondere; Canti Barocchi
(Mondadori, Milan, 1960); reprinted 1967.

Plumelia (Scheiwiller, Milan, 1967).

Library of Congress Card: 74-37576

ISBN: 0-691-06227-7

Publication of this book has been aided
by the Louis A. Robb Fund

This book has been composed in Linotype Electra
with Stradivarius display type

Printed in the United States of America
by Princeton University Press

COLLECTED POEMS OF

TRANSLATED AND EDITED BY
BRIAN SWANN AND RUTH FELDMAN

WITH A FOREWORD BY GLAUCO CAMBON
AND AN AFTERWORD BY EUGENIO MONTALE

PRINCETON UNIVERSITY PRESS
PRINCETON, NEW JERSEY · 1972

TRANSLATORS' INTRODUCTION

LUCIO PICCOLO presents a special difficulty for the translator. At first glance, however complex the syntax or elusive the thought, he seems old-fashioned, even *fin-de-siècle*, fantastically and arcanely baroque. And yet, further acquaintance reveals that his main thrust is post-existential ("anxiety" is a key word): that, for instance, in his constant search to distinguish outer and inner reality, he has affinities with such a conjurer as Nabokov. His efforts to describe consciousness are of a piece with Nabokov's attempt in *Ada* to encompass "the Texture of Time."

Thus, although Piccolo is typically solid and specific in his task, at times the Italian almost floats away in a Roethkean "shift of things." In these translations, we have attempted to retain the numinous, though occasionally we have not hesitated to "clarify" a few complex passages which came out unsatisfactorily in English. That is, we have followed the lead of W. H. Auden who, in his Preface to Dag Hammarskjöld's *Markings*, notes that obscurity raises a special problem for the translator who should, in difficulty, "write an intelligible English at the cost of altering what the original text actually says." We trust, however, that we have not *altered* anything: that any reconstructing is true to the spirit of the original phrase.

We have doubtless not escaped the opprobrium traditionally reserved for the translator, the *traduttore-traditore*. Yet we have aimed at producing poems intended to be judged as viable in their own right; as experiences comparable to the original, speaking with power in another tongue. English, of course, is often inadequate in expressing certain Italian forms. For instance, Latin languages are more persuasive in their abstractions—large, rotund-sounding, and authentically awe-inspiring. English, in its modern pragmatic stance at least, seems to take less easily to such habits, and so we have rung the changes on "soul," "anxiety," "yearnings," and the rest wherever possible. Even with such minimal allowances, however, we feel that Piccolo in English, like Poe in French, takes on real authority.

Two final matters. First, the question of collaboration, and here Borges has perhaps said the last word. In "An Autobiographical Essay" he writes: "I have often been asked how collaboration is possible. I think it requires a joint abandoning of ego, of vanity, and maybe of common politeness. The collaborators should forget themselves and think only in terms of the work." As far as the present work goes, we might add that it is a synthesis in every way. Each phrase is the product of two minds.

Finally, we owe immense debts to a large number of people, generous friends with specialized knowledge. This book would not have been possible without the original suggestion of the project by Masolino d'Amico, and his subsequent aid and encouragement. The book has profited much from the perspicuity and fine generosity of Luigi G. Jacchia and Sergio Perosa, and the advice of Liliana Burgess, Matilde Pfeiffer, Arturo Vivante, and Anna Yona moved the book through many difficult passages. We are grateful also to Gioacchino Lanza Lampedusa, Duke of Palma, and the executors of the Piccolo estate; to the Baronessa Agata Giovanna Piccolo; to Vittorio Sereni of Mondadori; and to Glauco Cambon.

ACKNOWLEDGMENTS

Acknowledgments are due to the following journals for extending hospitality to certain poems appearing in this volume:

Antaeus ("The Sundial," "The Soul and Sleights of Hand," "The Three Figures").
Chelsea ("The Suburbs").
Forum Italicum ("The Dead," "The Street Outside the Gate," "Plumelia").
The Journals of Pierre Menard ("Where Sun-Spores").
The Literary Review ("Shadows," "At the Time of the Bourbon King," "Patrol," "Although You Seek").
The Malahat Review ("Candles").
The Mediterranean Review ("Sirocco," "We Live by Pauses").
Poetry ("The Days").
Poetry Review ("The Hunt," "Inconstant World," "But in the Night that Crosses," "Long Tendrils").
Quarterly Review of Literature ("Hide and Seek," "Night," "The Moon Brings the Months," "The Warning").
Texas Quarterly ("The Oven," "The Farmhouse," "Veneris Venefica Agrestis").

Acknowledgments are also due to Arnoldo Mondadori Editore, publishers of *Gioco A Nascondere, Canti Barocchi E Altre Liriche,* and to Edizioni di Vanni Scheiwiller, publishers of *Plumelia.*

CONTENTS

Hide and Seek (1960)
(FOR EUGENIO MONTALE)

Baroque Songs and Other Lyrics (1956)

Plumelia (1967)
(FOR ANTONIO PIZZUTO)

COLLECTED POEMS OF
LUCIO PICCOLO

LUCIO PICCOLO, A FOREWORD

BY GLAUCO CAMBON

I first heard of Lucio Piccolo from Eugenio Montale in 1955, before the publication of *Baroque Songs*, and the air of secret surprise in the established poet's fireside talk when describing his visit with the then unknown fellow-artist still hovers for me around the late Sicilian baron's work. The published part of it amounts to three thin volumes of verse: *Canti Barocchi* (*Baroque Songs*) of 1956, *Gioco a Nascondere* (*Hide and Seek*) of 1960, and *Plumelia* of 1967. Nine poems had previously been privately printed in Palermo, as a booklet which was to become part of the later Milan publications. Obviously this was no prolific writer, though his vastly belated debut on the Italian literary scene (at fifty-three years of age!) probably implies tireless decades of private writing and erasing, if we consider the polished quality of what he finally deemed worthy of appearing in print. An eccentric erudite, Piccolo came and went like a man born too late to reap the recognition he deserved, and his legacy marks him as a maverick of modern Italian poetry, with all the drawbacks such a distinction entails in a country not overly ready to take its intellectual outsiders to its heart.

For the literary climate in postwar Italy scarcely favored unchallenged success for poets of Lucio Piccolo's stripe. Politically committed verse, neofuturist avant-garde, a generally iconoclastic temper tended to reject gentler practitioners of

3

the art or to insulate them in a limbo. "Hermetic" finesse was either suspect or passé, even in the eyes of some of its former devotees. No wonder that Piccolo's cultivated, if elvish, muse had to strike ideologically oriented readers as anachronistic. He must have felt the sting pretty acutely, to judge from the recently published fragment "Un Osso Duro" ("A Hard Bone," *Fiera Letteraria*, September 26, 1971), an outburst against supposedly prejudiced detractors and ignorers. A similar fate beset his cousin and kindred spirit Giuseppe Tomasi di Lampedusa, whose novel *The Leopard* aroused the fierce hostility of some eminent writers of fiction because of its anti-historical, reactionary, nuance-prone attitude which flew in the face of both democratic ideas and experimental aesthetics. Piccolo's reception was less turbulent, it is true, and he never knew the kind of popularity Lampedusa obtained on the commercial level; but this is what you would expect from a poet in verse.

His non-historical stance matches Lampedusa's entropic sense of time, a typically Sicilian heritage enhanced in the two exceptional kinsmen by their common aristocratic lineage. Time for them is entropy because it can only consume, never produce. Utopia, if at all thinkable, is a thing of the past, not of the future. In view of this it pays to ponder Piccolo's strange similarity to Theodore Roethke, a poet who, I am sure, never actually "influenced" him, no matter how familiar he may have become with the American's work through some of the several anthologies of American verse that saw the light in postwar Italy. Themes and technique partly correspond. Roethke keeps fancying a lost childhood which is the key to a sheltering, motherly, magical universe,

4

so much so that one could apply to it the notion of "pre-existence" so incisively formulated by Hugo von Hofmannsthal a few decades earlier, as the ultimate goal of the poet's quest for innocence. Likewise, minimal as well as large-scale cosmic events register on Piccolo's wonderstruck alertness with the timeless prestige of fairy tale; his surprise at nature's pageantry (which reabsorbs all man's works) wavers between childlike communing and childlike eavesdropping. In Piccolo's case, however, I feel inclined to replace the notion of "pre-existence" with "post-existence," if this coinage be allowed to stand for the Sicilian's kind of post-historical consciousness which partly overlaps with, and partly offsets in neat symmetry, the pre-historical orientation of Roethke. For history appears in *Baroque Songs* and in the later books as sybilline mementoes; the sundial, in the poem of that title, makes a fit emblem for the poet's consciousness steadily scanning the protean whirlpool of phenomena. As in Roethke, anguish balances rapture; the perception of universal flux loosens or dissolves the patterns of traditional meter into open, waving free rhythms which accumulate breathlessly to suggest trance. "The Sundial," one of Piccolo's most memorable pieces, sharply climaxes this crescendo with the abrupt conclusion:

> ... se l'attimo è sgomento
> l'eterno è terrore.

> ... if the fleeting is dismay
> eternity is terror.

A weird lucidity emerges from rapture; the rhythmic shape of the poem perfectly embodies its emblematic import.

It is just this component of anguished lucidity that rescues Piccolo's poetics from the sensuous abandon of D'Annunzio (an antecedent duly noticed by Piccolo's discoverer, Montale). It would not have been inconceivable for our Southern aristocrat to be lured into Dannunzian epigonism, since D'Annunzio was the first to experiment with the long sentence and wavy open line which paved the way for later innovators in Italian poetry, Montale included. Montale himself, I suspect, was Piccolo's chief antidote against that danger. I can overhear Montalian cadences in quite a few of *Baroque Songs* and in *Plumelia*, though it would never occur to me to call Piccolo an imitator of Montale. The ability to learn from a major artist without succumbing to him is a sure test of artistic power, and this test is one that Lucio Piccolo certainly passed. See for instance his lavish use of hidden rhyme. That comes straight from Montale's first book (*Cuttlefish Bones*, 1925); so does the emphasis on a low-keyed conversational utterance which keeps shifting from the standard hendecasyllable line (the Italian stepchild of Latin iambic pentameter) to uncanonical longer lines or to canny conglomerates of shorter metric units, and alternately to brief single lines. All of this helps to establish the persona's tone, the insinuating shape of the voice, as a piece like "Sirocco" can show with its resilience and chromatic richness which invite comparison with Montale's "English Horn" and "Tramontana" ("North Wind").

Here and elsewhere ("Sundial," "Night," "Veneris Venefica Agrestis," "Anna Perenna," to name a few exemplary compositions) Piccolo pulls all the stops of his resourceful instrument. It does seem fair to point out that he always strikes his own note, and it is a peculiarly southern, indeed baroque, one. More decidedly than in the early and middle Montale, it is the phrase that engenders rhythm. Piccolo is a syntactical poet; with him clause generates clause, sentences and images proliferate, and (particularly in the first book) hidden rhymes vie and interlock with standard end-rhymes to intone a symphony of multiple echoes, indeed to minimize the independence of individual lines and wrench the set patterns within which the musical stream sometimes flows. Piccolo's phrase overflows the dams of fixed meter; formal limits are there only to be transgressed. This exuberance, which asserts itself both on the rhythmical and on the iconic level, is Piccolo's signature, and it may have put off readers bent on verbal hardness, on sharp definition and cutting statement.

A signally unfashionable poet at the time of his first epochal publication in 1956, he remained so to the end. In times so addicted to topical or polemical relevance, it was easy to suspect him of verbal complacency, and the introspective vein was no longer part of the mainstream; it sent one back to the "Crepuscolari" poets of the years before World War I. But Piccolo is too gaudy—in his funereal Sicilian way—to fit the "crepuscular" label completely. For that matter, Brian Swann's uneasy use, in his Translators' Introduction, of the term "baroque" itself shows how intractable such labels can be even when useful, in the presence of such an elusive poetry. But then, baroque style did not die out with the seventeenth century, and if Piccolo is neobaroque, so were Hart Crane and Ungaretti, so is Bartolo Cattafi, a younger Sicilian contemporary. In fact, Piccolo shares with his ancestors of Góngora's age that supreme concern for the instability of phenomena which makes life a phantasmagoria—an inexhaustible, yet deceptive richness under which nothingness yawns. Poems on inconstancy were common in the baroque age; Nature's sleight-of-hand performance prompts Piccolo to write his prose-poem on the stage magician who becomes submerged in his own legerdemain and, as artist, indistinguishable from Nature's phantom creativity. The playing cards which, Alice-like, walk into the Sicilian landscape to blend with it (in the poem that follows, "Cards on the March") offer one poignant variation on that theme. The craftsman rivals Nature itself as master of metamorphoses. The epic of "undecipherable" water luxuriates in an avalanche of imagery—to focus in the voracious eye of the sundial, unmentioned but dominant like the mind of the poet who has seen through the tides of appearance and pierced the veil of Maya: "if the fleeting is dismay/ eternity is terror."

To such a disabused mind, what can history mean? Piccolo's writing, I insist, expresses a post-historical consciousness, because he seems to inhabit a world where everything already happened long ago, where history can only regress to folklore, shadow, sorcery. The Bourbon monarchs who were dethroned by Garibaldi in 1860 are as shadowy as the playing-card kings and queens parading in some of the poems; the Moorish invaders of long-forgotten centuries are now encapsulated in a metaphor like "la torma moresca dei venti," the Moorish band of winds let loose on the embattled island; the hermit who left his traces on the mountain to be scaled in the first of the nine *Plumelia* pieces rises from racial memory as mere ghost to burn again like sinister fireworks in the untold catastrophe which seems to consummate all of history. History is madness, then, and the past is the murmuring shades of the dead who haunt the crumbling corridors of many a mansion. Folksong or nursery-rhyme refrains ring out in some of the lyrics. The generative force of Nature is personified in an anti-Venus, "Veneris venefica agrestis," a fitful witch whose works and theater are all of Sicily. These incantations remind me of Dylan Thomas' Druidic Wales. Regressive time, a geology of the soul, persists as individual doom. Nothing more can happen, only fable is possible now, to the death.

Piccolo's poetry, of clearly consummate craftsmanship, did not change much through the final years, unless we want to take into account *Plumelia's* somewhat drier diction. In what sense it would have developed if Piccolo had lived longer, it is hard to say. We can only say that it was another of those improbable Sicilian gifts to the literature of Italy and Europe, a gift against the grain, from the island of Pirandello and Lampedusa and Quasimodo, the island of volcanic paradox. The supple versification has enabled Brian Swann and Ruth Feldman to find such a persuasive English music for Piccolo's text that I must call them his peer conjurers—now that he himself needs to be conjured. In Piccolo's words, as translated by them, "a measure flexible and strong."

Storrs, Connecticut
November 1971

9

GIOCO A NASCONDERE
ad Eugenio Montale

HIDE AND SEEK
for Eugenio Montale

Gioco a Nascondere

Quando comincia, quando finisce
il gioco non sappiamo, forse
era giorno ... ma solo che dentro
o fuori è poco diverso,
dentro su trame di passaggi,
di corridoi, di scale, fuori
tra i vapori del giorno
sommerso e cascame di luna;
una misura flessibile e forte
veloce e cauta ci ha preso, ci porta
su per le rampe di scaloni,
via senza peso per anditi a volo—
e fuori sono i covoni, il pagliaio
il fieno che respira denso,
l'aria immota che tenta
dalle aiole verbena o datura ...
e girano, tornano i viali
su fondi di tempi sospesi
fra sogno e memoria;
                     oscillare
elastico tra due piatti
di bilancia, uno verso le radici
del buio: le cantine, l'altro
in alto, in alto, dietro
la finestra che dà
sui tetti, ove senti vicine
la notte le stelle a guardare

Hide and Seek

When the game starts, when it ends
we don't know, perhaps
it was day . . . except there's little
difference inside or out,
inside over the weft of passages,
corridors, staircases, outside
among the mists of submerged
day and moonshreds;
a measure flexible and strong
quick and cautious has seized us, carries us
up great flights of stairs,
and weightless away—
and outside are sheaves, a strawrick,
hay with its dense breath,
the still air that lures
verbena or datura from the flower beds . . .
and garden paths turn, return,
suspended between dream and memory,
above times' depths;
                              to swing
elastic between two pans
of a balance, one toward the roots
of darkness, the cellars: the other
up high, high, behind
the window that gives
onto the roofs, where, as you gaze
by night, you feel stars

(un crepitio!) e di giorno
si stendono piani rigati
di strade, ponti, rocche, fiumare
di vetro, lontani poggi, marine. . .
Se noi siamo figure
di specchio che un soffio conduce
senza spessore né suono
pure il mondo dintorno
non è fermo ma scorrente parete
dipinta, ingannevole gioco,
equivoco d'ombre e barbagli,
di forme che chiamano e
negano un senso—simile all'interno
schermo, al turbinio che ci prende
se gli occhi chiudiamo, perenne
vorticare in frantumi
veloci, riflessi, barlumi
di vita o di sogno
—e noi trascorriamo inerti spoglie
d'attimo in attimo, di flutto in flutto
senza che ci fermi il giorno
che sale o la luce che squadra le cose.
*

                         Ma il gioco
è nulla in sé, soltanto che ci rende
vigili al secondo e fa
che vibrino le fibre, i diaframmi celati
(favole di batticuore ai boschi,
d'inseguimenti, di dogane eluse)
scorriamo ai margini
di mobili ellissi, d'aeree spirali

close to you (sputtering!),
and by day flat land stretches out striped
with roads, bridges, citadels, rivers
of glass, distant hills, seascapes. . . .
If we are mirror-images
a breath blows
without substance or sound
the world around us
is not stable either but a fleeting
painted wall, deceitful game,
equivocal with shadows and glares,
and forms that evoke
and deny a meaning—like the screen
within us, the whirling that seizes us
if we close our eyes, endless
spinning in swift
fragments, reflections, gleams
of life or of dream—
and we pass, inert sloughings
from moment to moment, wave to wave
without being stopped by dayrise,
or light that delineates.
*

                                                        But the game
is nothing in itself, only
it makes us aware of each second
and tenses fibres and hidden diaphragms
(stories of breathtaking chases
in woods, customsmen eluded)
we glide on the edges
of moving ellipses, airy spirals

ai pericoli che il buio
configura, e la casa
vive d'un respiro
diverso (non sapevamo
di tante curvature
in cui s'apre a proteggere)
oscura mormora, pende
immenso giroscopio,
palpita d'orientamenti
ignorati, si concentra, s'aggroviglia,
poi d'improvviso si distende in piani
esitanti, in fuggenti gallerie,
tetti morti ove il Vento
restò nascosto ed ha
sciami segreti ai fori, ai cannicci
e trae fievoli fiati dalle gravi travature,
scala a vite che sali
sali e spiri
come un fischio
in esili giri di correnti
d'aria,
terrazza su le tegole
che navighi le notti di maestrale;
*

        ed ora alla ricerca
d'un punto ove lo spazio s'aggomitoli
che sia soltanto noi, ma un grido
spezza il cerchio, precipita lo spazio
di nuovo invade . . .
           volti fittizi

to the dangers that darkness
shapes, and the house
breathes with a different
breath (we did not know
it opened into so many
sheltering curves),
murmurs darkly, hangs,
a huge gyroscope,
throbs with unknown
orientations, gathers itself, tangles,
then suddenly stretches into hesitant
planes, into fugitive galleries,
dead rooftops where the wind
lay hidden and keeps
secret swarms in holes, in the reed-wattle,
and draws feeble breaths from the heavy roofbeams,
spiral stairs you climb,
climb and expire
like a hiss
in thin twists
of air,
terrace on the tiles
that navigates nights of the mistral.
*
                              and now to the search
for a point where space curls up
to be us alone. But a cry
shatters the circle, throws space headlong
invades anew . . .
                    sham cardboard

di cartone o tessuto ai nascondigli
dalla mano incontrati ove li esplora,
fantocci a condizione
di buio e ingombri cadono sfiorati
e s'afflosciano in pieghe di tendaggi
privi d'osso e contorni;
pertugi, sgabuzzini, ambienti
nascosti tra le quinte
dove monomania
di specchi in ombra accolse i sedimenti
d'epoche smorte, di fasi sbiadite,
che il riflusso dei giorni in un torpore
lasciò fuori del sole:
perplessa civetta di crino
in attesa d'un varco
non permesso nel vivo,
minorata suppellettile, cappello
forato, a tuba, ventagli,
soffietto che non sai piú respirare,
fronzoli di gale spettrali
o di lutti perenti che un filo
di ragno ancora tiene
al tempo grigio degli ingrandimenti
—dimenticata
fu nella boccia la medicina . . .
e sul torbo crepuscolo verdigno
si levarono branche vacillanti
dall'immonda palude, molli
efflorescenze a galla, fronde . . .
ma da queste congiure

or cloth faces in hideaways
found by the probing hand,
puppets dependent on darkness
and clutter fall wilted,
droop like folded drapery,
boneless, shapeless;
narrow passages, lumber rooms, places
hidden in the wings
where monomania
of mirrors in shadow stored the dregs
of wan epochs, of washed-out phases,
which day's ebbing left in a torpor
out of the sun:
puzzled stuffed owl
waiting for a way out
denied in life,
disabled furniture,
riddled top hat, fans,
bellows you can no longer blow,
frills of spectral finery
or of bygone mourning that a spider's
thread still holds
to grey enlargements—
medicine
forgotten in a bottle . . .
and in the muddy greenish twilight
wavering tentacles rose
from the foul swamp, soft
efflorescences on the surface, fronds . . .
but from these conspiracies

di malsani fermenti
ove perdura l'impronta
d'un dubbio o memoria maligna
s'addensa forse la larva
d'un destino sinistro:
si leverà quando vorrà la Notte
assunta su le volte
e le vegliarde e i fusi
daranno il segno
sui pendoli, ai quadranti acherontei.

*

Ma questa scialbatura d'un istante
agli androni ove ingolfano le rampe
con gli imperi di gesso chi la dà?
Sospetto che la luna
lontana e avvolta pure non tralascia
gli infiltramenti oltre le mura e pone
lenta bozzoli di bambagia,
matasse di filamenti di umori
albi e lo sa
la gonna appesa nel sonno di canfora . . .
(sconfinamento è il suo cammino
ora che questo limbo
ha ridonato fluidità di origini)
molle pantomima che fai sorgere
dalle pareti le figure:
le tonache di cenere, le vane
panoplie, vezzi
moine che incorniciano
su volti centenari cuffie

of unhealthy fermentings
where the imprint of a doubt
or a malign memory lingers,
perhaps the phantom
of a sinister destiny takes shape:
it will lift when night wishes
raised to the vaults
and the old women with their spindles
will give the sign
on the pendulums to the quadrants of Acheron.
*

But who gives this momentary
paling to the halls where staircases
are swallowed up with empires of plaster?
I suspect too the veiled and distant moon
does not fail to leave
its filterings beyond the walls
and slowly lays down cocoons of cotton,
skeins of white
vapors and the skirt
hung in a camphor sleep knows it . . .
(its way is a trespass
now that this limbo
has restored fluidity of origins).
Limp pantomime, you make
figures leap from the walls:
vestments of ashes, vain
panoplies, affected
smirks that plumed bonnets
frame on centenarians'

piumate, pendagli di nere giade . . .
ancora un luccichio
di mica hanno su l'elitre
delle vizze libellule l'estinte
capigliature!—interminati
corridoi di lenzuola—
di mosci camici spioventi,
di vesti appese cui non è concesso
il corpo che le fa increspare
forse solo una maschera . . . bisnonne
impensate da scale d'anni,
scendono senza passi ora: fruscii,
blandizie che dànno il brivido, e pure
un senso familiare d'oltre il limite
(non hanno che una piega ed un riflesso).
E queste oscillazioni? Cerca
una sua fase il tempo, e se uno specchio
si svela ci riflette
come fummo o saremo; volti
trascorrono, cui diedero un contorno
l'ansia, l'ignoto . . . ora ci guardano
volti senza memoria né rilievo
—se non un guizzo—che sapemmo già
vita nel sole: simulacri
d'altri (o di noi?) che sono lontananze
irrimediate se li sfiori,
ed è l'impronta un esile risveglio
di dolore o incolpevole rimorso,
forme che la marea
fatue sospinse

faces, pendants of black jade . . .
the dead tresses
still have the mica sparkle
of withered dragonflies' wings!—
interminable
corridors of sheets—
of slack drooping smocks,
dresses hung up not granted
a body to crease them:
perhaps only a disguise . . . unthought-of
great-grandmothers now descend from
staircases of years without steps: rustlings,
caresses that make one shiver,
and even a familiar sense of beyond the limit
(they have only a fold and a reflection).
And these fluctuations? Time
seeks its own phase, and if a mirror
is unveiled it reflects us
as we were or will be; faces
flit by, their contours fixed
by anxiety, the unknown . . . now faces
watch us without memory or features—
only a flickering—faces we once knew
alive in the sun: semblances
of others (or of us?), irreparably
distant should you graze them,
their imprint a faint awakening
of grief or blameless remorse,
fatuous forms
which the tide drove

tra fuggevoli lumi
verso l'orbita d'ombra
che ventila d'intorno . . .
ai fiocchi vizzi delle sete
pendono le chitarre,
remoto è il mondo, bigio, inafferrabile.

*

Ora è la volta delle stanze, dei luoghi che non esistono, quelli che vengono su ad istanti, di sbiego, e sono sempre dove si è cessato di guardare o non si guarda ancora proiezioni e riflessi in un prolungamento dello spazio vengono fuggevoli a galla nei sogni del sonno o in quelli che scorrono incessanti in noi e solo a momenti sentiamo: la scala non cessa lassú al pianerottolo sotto il lucernale, s'apre sul muro la porta d'un altro appartamento—oh la scarsa luce dalle imposte accostate, il respiro d'inchiostro disseccato, la polvere dei libri e del tarlo, i copia-lettere oppressivi—è il parente di generazioni piú addietro mai esistito se non forse in una fotografia (ch'era d'un altro!) avvizzita.

Cosí una sera, spenti ancora i lumi, il coperchio d'una stufa coi suoi trafori chiamò l'ingresso d'una fuga di stanze su la parete.

*

E il gioco si prolunga
e il gioco non ha fine,
al nascondiglio segue
subito scoprimento,
(bolle d'aria emergiamo
su per l'albe polari
del lucernale . . .) batte

24

through ephemeral lights
toward the orbit of shadow
that flutters about us . . .
guitars hang
from faded silk tassels,
the world is remote, gray, ungraspable.
*

Now it's the turn of the rooms, of places that don't exist, those that appear at moments, all awry, and are always where you have stopped looking or aren't looking as yet, projections and reflections in an extension of space surface fleetingly in dreams of sleep or in those that flow unceasingly in us and are only sensed at moments: the staircase does not end up there at the landing, under the skylight, the door of another apartment opens in the wall—oh the dim light from the closed shutters, the breath of dried ink, the dust of books and woodworm, the burdensome copying-press and the relative of earlier generations who never existed except perhaps in a yellowed photograph (of someone else!)

Thus, one evening, with lights still out, the perforated stove-lid summoned up the entrance of a fugue of rooms on the wall.
*

And the game goes on
and the game has no end,
hiding gives way
to sudden discovery
(bubbles of air we rise
through the skylight's
polar dawns . . .), it beats

leggero di nuovo nell'alto,
scivola nell'interno
penetrale, e sale attraversate
baluginanti di marmi
pendenti di cristalli
o di sibille assorte
nei manti dei portali,
girano come chiatte
sovra il perno dell'ombra,
(uno spettro di stagnola
al gesto d'un fanale
striscia si frange è spento)
slungati a dismisura
sotto un divano sorgiamo
nastro esiguo, non visti
sentiamo come i morti,
o come la foglia grande
triangolare che sbuca
dai velari dell'aria
(convergenti occhi di vuoto
bocca d'un taglio)
che gira sospesa un momento
gira guarda e dispare,
e il passo è sempre piú
veloce, tutt'uno con le pareti
col respiro polveroso
dei tappeti, scorre l'inafferrata
farandola, la ridda
vana che non ha centro,
e quello ch'era strillo

lightly again high up,
slips to the innermost
recess, and rooms traversed
glittering with marbles,
hung with crystals,
or pensive sibyls
in the hangings of the great doors,
turn like barges
above the pivot of darkness
(at a lantern's movement
a tinfoil ghost glides
shatters dies),
elongated beyond measure
we rise, a thin ribbon,
from under a divan, unseen
we feel like the dead,
or like the big triangular
leaf that issues
from curtains of air
(converging eyes of emptiness
mouth of a cut)
that twists suspended a moment,
whirls, looks about, and disappears,
and the pace is always
faster, at one with the walls
with the dusty breath
of rugs, the elusive
farandola glides by, the reel
that has no center,
and what was a playful

di gioco ora è terrore . . .
di minuto in minuto
s'attende che dal muto
sbadiglio dello stipo
socchiuso si levi l'archetto
del nero contrabasso . . .
Ma in questa fuga dal mondo illusorio
ch'eludere vuole lo spazio
in alto, in alto s'è disciolto un nodo
di limpidi astri che teneva ascoso
il nuvolame, e splende e oscilla:
una dolce lampada di riposo
brucia ancora per noi sul promontorio?

shriek is now terror . . .
minute by minute
one waits for the bow
of the black double-bass
to rise from the silent yawn
of the half-closed cabinet. . . .
But in this flight from the illusory world
that wishes to elude space,
high up, a node of limpid
stars hidden by clouds
is freed, shines and sways:
a soft harbor-light
still burns for us on the promontory?

Anna Perenna

Sul tetto
subito s'alza, sovrasta il monte—
ingombro a manca di dumoso
verde su verde, di coltri di sfatto
fogliame, di cortecce vetuste, di sterpi—
e il cappero, l'euforbia, pendono alle venture
dei venti; dove volge la costa
e chiama l'ombra e la stende sugli increspamenti,
al dorso della salita s'aprono pieghe,
conche di verde piú denso, s'indovina
vescia, ranuncolo, porro, su foglia
spessa, su bronchi carponi, schiuma,
saliva di bosco, oscura rugiada di gambo
tumido, di spino, di gozzo di fusto
che trasuda, quel ch'è viscido d'iridi, che mai
vede sole (e assidue le invisibili spole
tessono, mutano, ma il giro è sempre lo stesso)
nutrito d'umido antico, di vegetale ruggine . . .
e forse sfugge la lucertola senz'occhi . . .
                    Ma dove lo spacco
fende il fianco alla montagna
giú da barbe pendenti, da penduli rovi gromme
(configura la creta cavi antichissimi volti in discesa,
in frana lenta spioventi)
giú per lunghe decrepite rughe a doccia
s'accolgano stillanti—scende

Anna Perenna

                              Above the rooftop
suddenly the mountain climbs, looms—
encumbered on the left with spiny
green on green, blankets of rotting
leaves, ancient bark, dry twigs—
and the caper, the spurge, hang at the winds'
caprice; where the coast swerves
and summons shadow and spreads it on the ripplings,
hollows unfold on the slope's crest,
pockets of a deeper green, you guess
at puff-ball, buttercup, wild leek, on the thick
leaf, on creeping scrub, scum,
wood spittle, dark dew of the swollen
stalk, of thorn, of oozing
bole-tumor, that which is slimy with rainbows, that never
sees the sun (and the invisible shuttles, assiduous,
weave, change, but the circuit is always the same)
nourished by ancient damp, vegetable rust . . .
and maybe the eyeless lizard darts away . . .
                              But where the cleft
splits the mountain's flank
down from dangling beards, trailing brambles, incrustations
(clay outlines hollow primeval faces descending,
flowing in a slow landslide)
down through long worn creases like waterspouts
drops collect—

ripido bianco liquido nastro
a saetta, frigge all'intoppo
vitrea verga eguale suona
da lubriche lastre di roccia
oriolo d'ore solitarie: i gradini
nella pietra, la conca dove spicca
goccia dopo goccia e l'orciolo attende, branca
di sughero che tenta varcare di nuvola
da cima a cima scia di silenzio—il merlo
che salta sullo stecco del perastro
dà tre note, poi sale più alto,
il fuscello minimo che gira gira
vira e dispare dove fa gomito canale di solco.
E i mesi hanno il loro gioco: ventata
dirompe balze di nuvolaglia, s'apre,
turbina, palpita, celeste vortice, chiama
pensieri e foglie—umido poi, sensitivo
gronda dalle tegole, lascia che lo prenda
pozza d'acqua, che lo distenda
diramatura di torrenti
verso il vespero tardivo;
poi si sciolgono nei sogni figure . . .
Marzo, le notti, accende vive
candele di cristallo, marzo prodigo d'orizzonti
che sfiora le timide sorgive;
aprile, insensibile ancora
filtra nei crepuscoli glabri
tacito scorre, cresce, gonfia
bitorzolo d'erba, vescica di luna
ch'era nei boschi celata ed ora
obliqua storta distillerà il tempo

a steep white liquid ribbon
arrows down, seethes at obstacles,
a glassy rod makes the same sound
from slippery slabs of rock
clock of solitary hours: the steps
in the stone, the rock basin where drop
after drop detaches and the jug waits, claw
of cork-oak that tries to cross
from cloudpeak to cloudpeak a wake of silence—the
                                        blackbird
that hops onto the dry stick of the wild pear
sings three notes, then climbs higher,
the tiniest sprig that twists twists
veers and disappears where the furrow's channel forms an
                                        elbow.
And the months have their own game: a gust
breaks cloud-crags, bursts open,
whirls, throbs, celestial whirlwind, summons
thoughts and leaves—then sensitive damp
streams from the rooftiles,
lets a puddle of water draw it in,
a branching of streams extend it
toward tardy evening;
afterwards figures dissolve in dreams . . .
March, at night, kindles
live crystal candles, March prodigal with horizons
that lightly touches the timid springwater;
April, as yet imperceptible,
filters through slick twilights,
flows silently, grows, swells
the grass-clump, the moon-bladder

delle notti, l'ore di crescenze in ascolto—
meticoloso erborista insinua colori, prepara
ebollizioni ai fornelli, travaglio al mortaio,
la treccia secca che pende, il sambuco
l'origano polveroso, odoroso . . .
E maggio, giugno li chiude
tutti nel suo cerchio la rosa.
Ti vide qualcuno, Perenna, che protendevi
la lampada verso la catasta
del tramonto ad attingere il fuoco
quando sono di cremisi i vetri
d'occidente (ma la tua lampada brucia
alla fiamma d'ogni stagione) e sarà
nella notte ai lontani segnale
di favola e riposo; a una mossa
su lo spigolo, su la spalliera
saranno alle pareti la lepre
inseguita, congiure di manti e cappucci . . .
intese hai con l'ombra, Perenna,
urgono ad un tuo sguardo d'intorno
forze di generazioni inesauste
alle soglie, in ansia di forme
e passano sul tuo specchio
il Serafino e la Ruta;

                  a lungo sentimmo
un concentrarsi di nembi
luminosi nell'alto, il tuono tacito di fulgore,
poi la luce franò, colò su le cortecce dai frutteti
celesti in grappoli, in corimbi,
non fermarono i fusti tanto

the woods hid and which now,
askew, bent, will distill nights'
time, the hours of listening growth—
the meticulous herbalist insinuates colors, prepares
fomentations in retorts, toil at the mortar and pestle,
the dry braid that hangs, elder,
dusty oregano, fragrance-full . . .
And May, June, the rose
encompasses them all in its circle.
Someone saw you, Perenna, stretching
a lamp toward the sunset's pyre
to kindle the blaze
when the western windows are crimson
(but your lamp burns
at every season's flame) and at night
it will be a signal of fable and repose
to those far off; at a movement,
in the corner, on the chairback,
on walls there will be the hunted
hare, conspiracies of mantles and hoods . . .
you have secret understandings with the shadow, Perenna,
when you look around
unexhausted forces of generations crowd
against thresholds, yearning for forms
and the Seraph and the Rue
pass over your mirror;
                    for a long time we felt
a concentration of luminous
rainclouds overhead, the silent thunder of radiance,
then the light crashed, poured over the bark from heavenly

scorrere di cadenti corone:
si sciolse Giugno nell'aria.
Spanditi mese indora la crescenza del canto
se le parole lucide e sonore
ch'io prendo e ti traboccano
sono le tue ore, posso
figurarti in sembianze di giorni
ove l'aria ovunque è tepore
di piega, di lanugini, di sentori,
—e furono incontri di venti
ai crocevia rurali, soste d'aure
sui margini delle fontane,
lasciarono impronte
di leggerissime felci
sull'acqua, ripresero il volo;
e se le piogge notturne, a volte,
empirono le giare senza fondo dell'ombra
la terra si svegliò ch'erano molli
i sentieri e tutta sentiva
d'umide mandre al mattino,
e la rosa grave di gocce
fu specchio tremante alla nuvola furtiva,
e apparvero contrade
appiè di ripidi poggi
ove l'olivo, il fico d'India, l'agave
hanno per fondo dietro i cancelli
la zona che palpita di meriggio, il mare,
e sorgono, profondano i soli
nelle braccia infinite, giorni
che incendiano i raggi ogni atomo

orchards in bunches, clusters,
the tree-trunks did not halt such
a flow of cascading crowns:
June unfurled in the air.
Overflow, month, gild the crescendo of song!
If the lucid sonorous words
which I gather and which spill out of you
are your hours, I can
picture you in the features of days
when the air all about is the mild warmth
of a downy fold, scents,—
and there were encounters of winds
at country crossroads, pauses of breezes
on fountain-margins,
they left imprints
of very light ferns
on the water, resumed flight;
and if at times the night-rains
filled shadow's bottomless jars
the earth awoke and paths were
soft, everything smelled
of damp herds in the morning,
and the rose heavy with drops
was a tremulous mirror to the furtive cloud,
stretches of country appeared
below abrupt hills
where the olive, prickly pear, the aloe
have as background behind the gates
the zone that pulses with noon, the sea,
and suns rise, sink
into the infinite arms, days

d'aria, e l'aria solleva
balze, contrafforti di spume,
li frange in fulgore a scogliere . . .
vengono le storie del mondo
le muove dall'orizzonte
il vento che preme spazi all'udito;
ma tu pensi altre storie:
quelle che la notte fa bianche
di luce alla fronte dei colli;
ed anche il dolore, Perenna,
quasi non ferisce, colto
nella curva, sappiamo
ch'è la nota d'un canto,
tocca, si disperde in favola
mai creduta, ritorna
per disparire, ed a volte
sembra la vita un cammino
lungo alte coste eguale,
fra ombre di tamerici
nella luce di rame
del sole su le scogliere,
e solo dire, solo nel tardo
crepuscolo: l'umido scende
al ciglione dai monti, curvata
n'è l'erba, ne goccia il gradino,
la Notte alza fra due anse
di montagne lo stendardo
d'Orione su la vallata—
                    ma piú tardi, Perenna,
                              piú tardi

when beams set every atom of air
afire, and the air lifts
crags, foam buttresses,
breaks their refulgence on reefs . . .
the stories of the world come,
the wind that squeezes spaces against the ear
moves them from the horizon;
but you are thinking of other tales:
those which the night blanches
with light on the hills' brow;
even sorrow, Perenna,
scarcely wounds, gathered
in the curve, we know
it is the note of a song,
it touches, is dispersed in a fable
never believed, returns
to disappear, and at times
life seems a journey
along high even coasts,
among shadows of tamarisks
in the copper light of sun
on the reefs, is only
words, only in the late
twilight: dampness descends
on the mountainside, the grass
is bent there, the shelf drips with it,
between two loops of the mountains
Night hoists the standard
of Orion above the valley—
                    but later, Perenna,
                              later still

ancora chiedesti un papavero
ai giorni che dileguano
verso gli orizzonti sfocati?
Pungente è l'erba come i cardi
e fasci di giunchi alzarono alla fatica
delle ruote la polvere viva
e furono torbide e rossicanti
le lune d'Agosto all'attesa . . .

                              ora
(già due volte il torrente suonò le trombe,
fu tutto un tumulto
e rotearono cuffie di schiuma
in cima ai massi marmorei)

                    ora il mare, le notti,
è piú scuro e un'insenatura
v'è dove sempre tuona
anche s'è stellato e smorza il vento,
e su la coltre fallace
che scuote dal profondo
una forza misurata come di possenti reti
s'inseguono le campanelle d'acqua
s'infrangono . . . e l'onde
ai piedi dello scoglio ove schiocca
la sferza eguale gettano cerchi fuggevoli
ciarle di spume, solo il Carro
è verticale, ora la punta
del timone—un chiodo
di cristallo toccherà l'orlo ultimo—
ma nel chiuso
ov'errano sagome incerte

did you request a poppy
from days that vanish
toward unfocussed horizons?
The grass is prickly as thistles
and reed-bundles stirred live dust
at the wheels' laboring
and August moons were turbid
and red with expectation . . .

               now

(the torrent has already sounded its trumpets twice,
there was a great tumult
and coifs of foam spun
at the top of marbled masses)

               now the sea, the nights,

it is darker and there is an inlet
where it always thunders
even if it is starry and the wind dies down,
and on the deceptive pall
which a measured force as of powerful nets
shakes from the depths
bellflowers of water chase one another,
shatter . . . and at the reef's feet
where the regular whip-strokes crack, the waves
hurl fleeting circles, chattering spume;
only the Wain is vertical,
now the point of the shaft—
a crystal nail
will touch the outermost edge—
but in the enclosure
where blurred outlines roam

nei sogni, d'inerpicati dirupi,
d'erbe divelte, il respiro
in due sparte l'oscurità
e gli uberi teneri e forti
fanno umida la paglia ed i velli
i velli, Perenna, distesi
sono calmi nel sonno a la mano.

in dreams of precipices scaled,
of grass uprooted, the breath
divides darkness in two
and the tender strong udders
soak the straw, and the stretched fleeces,
the fleeces, Perenna,
are calm in sleep to the hand.

Il Forno

Non l'ho piú veduto brillare
a raffiche di firmamenti'
in fuga il forno, dal muro
forato, sospeso a un minuto,
nottetempo, fra scuro e scuro,
—dentro s'alzava furioso un vento
di sterpi in fuoco, una rissa—
poi riprendeva il sonno: l'errare
d'un viso d'un tempo d'un luogo
sommersi in un tempo indeciso;
anche di giorno chiamava
a immaginazioni, a sogni, di piú
se giornata piena di scontri
ventosi, di falchetti in alto, di galoppi
di nuvole su la schiena dei monti . . .
su dalle aperture
delle tegole figure da fumaioli
da tetti! accenni di braccia disperate,
di volti slungati di sgomento,
sfuggenti a sghembo da ruote
infrante, da vortici, e l'otre
che ballonzola a galla
nell'aria o allato a scope
viranti ventole spatole
sorte e disfatte
in uno sbuffo

44

The Oven

Never since have I seen the oven
glow with gusts of firmaments
in flight, from the pierced
wall, hung from a minute,
nighttime, between dark and dark—
within, a furious wind
of flaming wood, a riot—
then sleep returned: the roaming
of a face an hour a place
submerged in an unsettled time;
even by day it summoned us
to imaginings, dreams, the more so
if it was a day full of windy
collisions, hawks high overhead, clouds
galloping on the mountains' spine . . .
up from tiles'
apertures, from chimneys, roofs,
figures! beckonings of frantic arms,
faces lengthened by dismay,
receding obliquely from broken
wheels, vortices, and the wineskin
that bobs in
air or beside turning brooms,
fire-fans, spatula-shapes
made and unmade
in a puff

di fumo . . .
        figure
che crediamo sentire
anche nei desolati
tetti morti in cima a le scalette
di legno, ai lucernali,
quando batte, rimesta libeccio,
e in noi non hanno requie la notte.

Ma il fuoco non è sempre inferno:
se la bocca, fra ceppi gonfi
di fiamma era il disco
del sole mezzo immerso
nell'onde a canali, d'inverno,
fra cupi trionfi di nubi,
come prendeva cordiale di rosso
di corallo le gole lucide, calde,
gettate indietro all'alito delle vampate . . .
adorni di filigrane erranti le faville
sul corpetto slacciato, scosso, su le falde
delle gonne, su le braccia umide, a le vespe
in fuoco esche i capelli in minutissime treccie
nere o grigie, sparse a grani di scura spezie,
tutte crespe, stregonesche.
                Né il nero
è sempre maligno: virtú
sacrale di gesti, d'aspersioni, di lieviti
scesi da tempi e tempi e mano
che mesce mutano la vallata
adolescente di spighe, la sorgiva, le notti

46

of smoke . . .
                    figures
we believe we hear too
on the desolate
dead roofs at the head of the wooden
stairs, skylights
when the *libeccio* buffets, stirs again,
and they find no peace in us at night.

But the fire is not always inferno:
if the mouth, among flame-
swollen stumps was the sun's
disk, half sunk
in channeled waves, in winter,
among dark triumphs of clouds,
how coral-red cordial suffused
the gleaming warm throats
thrown back at the blaze's breath . . .
sparks, flickering filigree ornaments
on the unlaced agitated bodice, on skirt
folds, damp arms; to the fire-wasps
hair is tinder: tiny black or gray
braids, sprinkled with dark spice grains,
all frizzled, witchlike.
                    Nor is black
always malign: sacral
virtue of gestures, sprinklings, leavenings
descended from behind time, and the hand
that mixes, alter the valley
adolescent with wheat spikes, spring-water, nights

attente al gambo implume, i giorni di sola luce
in altra forma viva: il pane ch'esce
dall'antro infocato che lo matura
ora nella veste slargata delle ceste
di paglia e sotto i lini è carne
nuova che odora
per tanta carne che l'ha toccato.
                    Era l'interna
combustione da cui balzano i giorni
torbidi di fermenti inappagati
lanciati a roteare
fra boschi, riotte d'acqua e rupi;
salivano i mattini in cui profonda
pare la vita e rigida la luce
segna rilievi d'isole cretosi,
pensavamo i destini
snodarsi come strade
distese, pure se incomprese
rimasero le svolte . . . sopra il mondo
le sere si piegavano in sequenze
tacite d'ore, in blande
cadenze di memorie;
ma le fornaci, le querce,
gli attoniti volti rurali,
cortecce che la vampa incise
piú selvaggi, le notti di spettrali
incontri, le notti sospese
a un cadere d'acque lontane
—pareva che da tante attese
un'isola dovesse solitaria sorgere—

48

attentive to the unfledged stem, days of nothing but light
in another living form: the bread that issues
from the red-hot cave that ripens it
now in the swelling dress of straw
baskets and under linens is fresh
meat that smells
of all the flesh that has touched it.
                      It was the internal
burning from which spring the days
turbid with unsatisfied ferments
launched to whirl
among woods, brawling brooks and rocks;
mornings ascended in which
life seems profound and rigid light
traces the chalky outcrops of islands;
we thought our destinies
would unknot like stretched-out
roads, even if the windings
remained uncomprehended . . . above the world
evenings bowed in silent sequences
of hours, bland cadences
of memory;
but the furnaces, the oaks,
the stupefied country faces—
bark which flame carved
to more wildness, nights of spectral
encounters, night trailing
from a distant fall of waters—
it seemed a solitary island must rise
from so much waiting—

e quelle ancora
dove il cespuglio senza mossa d'aria
dava in aride risa . . . se sgomenti
di tanta trasparenza d'anni
di questo errare in attimi vediamo
tramezzi su invisibili rotaie
che trascorrono lungi e senza dove,
pure il suolo li serba e il suolo in noi
fermo è per sempre: il sonno che ci prende
grovigli ha d'erba, scorre il sibilio
delle stagioni al varco e nella cava
ha baleni il cristallo . . . né mai forza
può scemare a chi ascolta il suolo:
sarmenti in fuoco desti fra le rughe
montane quando a mezzo cielo
gira un gallo di nubi annunziatore
delle rustiche aurore sopra i colli
fra rovi e querce ignare . . .

and those nights too
in which the bush spilled arid laughter,
no air stirring . . . if, aghast
at such transparency of years,
at this wandering in moments we see
cross-ties pass far off
on invisible tracks going nowhere,
the very soil preserves them and the soil forever
remains within us: the sleep that overpowers us
is grass-tangles, the whistling
of the seasons flows to the gap,
and crystal flashes in the quarry . . . strength can never
wane in the man who listens to the soil:
lively twigs burning among
mountains' folds when, mid-sky,
a cloud-cock spins, harbinger
of rustic dawns above the hills
among brambles and imperceptive oaks . . .

Masseria

È forse per la cotogna
che nel frutteto pencola, odora
o forse per un altro frutto
tardo, che pende acceso
sull'ardesia fuggente del mare
tutto grinze di novembre,
già rosseggiante d'inverno?
   Ma nel passare
sul ponte, tra pioppi ad isole, vidi
la masseria a fianco delle fiumare
dove sembra che l'Anno incanti
le eguali immagini stagionali:
l'aratore gibbuto
che solca il suolo in pendio
—la saia d'acqua che scese
dall'alto e col suono incessante
la chiude in un sopore
di felci, d'eriche, su fondali
di nubi distese, di passeri in volo;
e senti vicine, davanti, l'ombre
delle stagioni, se un cenno le chiami:
scendono da le colline e le valli
le Primavere incostanti
di subiti rabbuffi, di cristalli
di pioggia e sole a le fronde raggianti;

The Farmhouse

Is it perhaps the quince
that dangles in the orchard, perfuming it,
or maybe another late
fruit that hangs glowing
over ocean's shifting slate,
wrinkled with November,
already turning red with winter?
              But crossing
the bridge, among poplar clumps, I saw
the farmhouse on the river's flank
where it seems the Year bewitches
the uniform seasonal images:
the hunched ploughman
who furrows soil on the slope—
the bunting of water that fell
from the heights and with incessant sound
encloses it in a torpor
of bracken, heather, on backdrops
of stretched clouds, passing sparrows;
and you sense close by, before you, the seasons'
shadows, if a sign evokes them:
the inconstant Springs
of sudden chidings, rain
crystals and sun with frond-like rays
descend from hill and valley;

gli Autunni venatori da le braci sommesse
che sui tetti stagnarono per sempre,
il riccio del castagno, e verde di burrasca
il borro ove mirare nelle pozze
un altro mese che s'allontana . . .
decantano le annate d'abbondanza
sotto le travi abbrunate, e quelle
di scarsezza pei segni che ritornano,
e la mano invisibile dell'aria
scosta la porta: è
l'ospite che conosci all'alito
d'orti montani . . . agli abbeveratoi
notturni, gravi di linfe, spessi
d'erranti nastri d'erbame,
i mantici dei buoi
ingoiano festuche sperse
riflessi d'astri . . . ed un folto
di mirti è a piè d'un colle
dove solo segno del tempo
è il trascorrere di nuvole su la cima
del declivio, frullo
di foglia che abbandona ramo
è il minuto, ed un altro
ne viene, e sono già lontani
parole d'una storia
senza inizio né fine;
e oscurano i soffitti
le notti dei racconti: "erano tre
nella caccia e li colse l'acquazzone,
poi fu tutto il crepuscolo un riflesso

hunting Autumns with their subdued embers
dried up on roofs forever,
the chestnut burr, and the ditch green with
squalls, in whose puddles
you see another month melt . . .
the fat years decant
under blackened beams, and the lean
years by recurrent signs,
and air's invisible hand
sets the door ajar: it is
the guest you know with a breath
of mountain gardens . . . in troughs
at night, heavy with sap, thick with
drifting skeins of greenstuff,
the bellows-jaws of oxen
greedily devour scattered straw,
reflections of stars . . . in a depth
of myrtles at the hill's base
the only evidence of time
is clouds coursing on the scarp's
crown, flutter
of a leaf abandoning a branch
is the minute, and another one
comes; already distant
are the words of a story
without beginning or end;
and ceilings darken
on nights of the story-telling: "there were three
out hunting and the cloudburst caught them,
then the whole twilight was a gleaming

vitreo di giacenti acque piovane
sotto boschive volte fra spioventi
ramaglie, tenue di larve
di fumi che salivano, vapori
vegetali esalati, verso
gli stinti alari d'occidente . . .

                              ma
la casa di fortuna che li accolse
sentiva d'anni, d'anime lontane,
e nella notte emersero (dai sogni?)
figure in ansia di reviviscenze
vietate, il nero
fornello che s'infiamma
d'antichi fuochi, familiari
enigmi paesani: il ticchettio
inesplicato al muro, timbri
aerei che un istante dissigilla
in murmure senza parole . . . uno
dei tre scambiò lo stipo per finestra,
e disse: come
scura è la notte, e sente di muffito!"
Ma nella stanza dove sempre fummo
anche se ci sfilarono dinnanzi
rombi di mondo, nella stanza
dove il battente ancora sente
di resina, di bosco, subito ritrovi
il coltello di legno, il regolo, la balestrina
che richiamava le navigazioni:
—sui mari boreali saettio
di scafi ischeletriti, vele

reflection of motionless rainwater
under wooded vaults among dripping
dead branches, tenuous with ghosts
of mounting smoke, exhaled
plant vapors, toward
the west's dimmed andirons . . .
                              but
the shelter they stumbled onto, which received them,
smelled of years, far-off souls,
and in the night figures emerged
(from dreams?) in a torment of forbidden
reawakenings, the black
stove that blazes with
ancient fires, familiar
country enigmas: the inexplicable
ticking in the walls, airy
tones an instant unseals
into a wordless murmur . . . one
of the three mistook the cabinet for a window,
and said: how
black the night is; it smells of mould!"
But in the room where we were all the time
even though rhombs of the world
unravelled before us, in the room
where the door still smells
of resin, of the woods, suddenly you find again
the wooden knife, the ruler, the small sextant
that recalled navigations:—
on northern seas flashing
of skeletal hulls, sails

che sfiorano incredibili
costellazioni . . .—le finestre
spiate a le fessure
nelle antiche tempeste
quando l'azzurro lampo tradiva il tuono . . .
il quadrato di cielo sovra i colli
solcato di cadenti
stelle tutta la notte
—le ritrovava l'alba lapilli
spenti fra l'erbe o lucenti
ghiaie fra i solchi—e non è trascorsa
l'ora al quadrante
che specchia i giri dell'Orsa;
sul tavolo ritrovi la candela
a mezzo consumata e la riaccendi
a riprendere le storie interrotte
che mai nessun giorno finiranno,
nemmeno quando tentenniamo al sonno,
e non è più ferma la cicogna
d'umido al muro, e ci prendono d'intorno
l'acque che scendono lungo la notte.

that graze incredible
constellations . . . —window
cracks peered through
in ancient tempests
when blue lightning betrayed thunder . . .
the square of sky above the hills
raked by falling
stars all night—
dawn found them spent
ash on grass or shining
gravel in the furrows—and the hour
on the quadrant
that reflects the Bear's turnings
is not past; on the table you find the candle
half consumed and relight it
to resume the interrupted tales
that will never finish,
not even when we nod off to sleep,
and the stork-shape of damp is no longer
steady on the wall, and the waters
that descend the length of night surround us.

Candele

Quando viene la tempesta bruciano le candele nella camera interna; per giungervi quanto passaggio di anditi, corridoi, tramezzi, gradini e scalette e il pavimento indiscreto che dà nota come un pedale d'organo, stridente, bassa, dall'armadio cavernoso.

Ma finalmente qui è il luogo della sicurezza, scavato nelle fibre delle mura di centro, nel cuore del riposo dove del mondo di fuori non arriva neppure la vibrazione d'un porta cenere al traino che passa, e il vento dei quadrivi e quello che corre intorno alle altissime gallerie sono soltanto lontano fantasma di sibilo.

E sembrano dimenticati i mappamondi polverosi i cristalli di zolfo nella coppa di vetro, al tempo che sulle pareti i pomeriggi battono celesti, tra le sbarre dell'inferriata è sciarpa che appena fluttua la marina, in un perpetuo addio, nella vasca l'acqua è mossa di sole e fronde, e sembra sopra i tetti e le terrazze che sempre eguale risuoni la stessa ora che il cielo immobile riassorbe; dietro le cime delle araucarie scivola la luna diurna verso i calmi padiglioni.

Ma qualcosa muta e quasi non ce ne avvediamo: scorre una nuvola sul disco del sole, l'acqua diviene a momenti argentina, poi è solcata come dal passaggio d'una schiera d'anitre invisibili; la ruota che dall'alto sembra spartire le luci diverse al giorno ha ora una misura diversa e dall'orizzonte e sul suolo tornano i colori ch'erano emigrati coi mesi.

Più tardi la finestra fu oscurata da foglie passeggere—e

Candles

When the storm comes, candles burn in the inner chamber: to reach it what a traversing of passageways, corridors, partitions, steps, staircases and the indiscreet floor that makes a sound like an organ pedal, harsh and bass, from the cavernous closet.

But here at last is the refuge, hollowed from fibres of the central walls, in the heart of stillness where not even the sound of an ashtray vibrating from a passing load penetrates from the world outside, and the wind from the crossroads and the one that sweeps around the highest galleries are only far phantoms of a hiss.

And dusty world maps, sulphur crystals in a glass beaker, seem forgotten when blue afternoons beat on the walls, between wrought-iron grilles sea is a scarf fluttering faintly in a perpetual farewell, in the basin water stirs with sun and leaves, and the same hour always seems to strike the same way above roofs and terraces and is reabsorbed by the motionless sky; behind tips of araucaria pines the day moon slips toward quiet pavilions.

But something mute and hardly perceptible: a cloud glides over the sun's disk, at moments the water turns silver, then furrowed as though a file of invisible ducks passed over; the wheel that seems to scatter varying lights to the day from above is now a different size and from the horizon colors that emigrated with the months return to the soil.

Later the window was darkened by flying leaves—and all

tutta notte alla vetrata batteva desolato il galletto di paglia.

E la tempesta viene: è tutto l'orizzonte marino che s'avvicina in una sola ondata sotto il cielo che grava, ha scavalcato gli antemurali, lanciato le schiume sabbiose ai colonnati in cerchio, ai portici, le alghe sono su le banchine, spinte quasi fino alle inferriate, alle aiole dove sui pilastri s'alzano le grandi urne cinerarie delle stagioni trapassate, dei giochi svaniti, dei passi nei viali; sono incandescenti e violetti gli acini dei grappoli neri d'acqua—su le pareti rispondono i coperchi di rame appesi, vetri d'armadi, e sono apparse sul muro lesioni, fessure, scabrosità, decrepitudine che non si sapevano, sui monti ora si curvano gli immensi uberi, le trombe degli elefanti in volo, sui crinali, su le creste, alle origini nascoste delle vallate e delle fiumare, gonfiano le arterie, le vene della terra.

Poi la strada suburbana diviene livida di fanghi, porta i cespi divelti e i rami, non vedrà il mandriano che staglia sul tramonto al passaggio delle pecore—fumano i mantelli al fuoco dello speco—e l'Avemaria cercherà in vano le bande di rosso e di viola che traversano i tratti neri dei voli.

E le candele bruciano e nulla è perduto ancora, stendono penombre e chiarori di pergamena, intimo volto di capezzale ad ogni cosa, e l'esitazioni come quando il sonno è per chiudere la cortina sul mondo—allora è sola la lampada la dolce soglia che cela la sua midolla in cerchi vacillanti, la passerella che fa serene le intermesse riprese, muta le insidie della macchia, le cadute nella botola, i terrori degli angoli nel respiro della radura, gli spaventi del pagliaio socchiuso nell'abete aereato dove giocano le campanelle della luna.

Ma quest'angoscia, quest'ansia?

night the straw cock beat desolate on the panes.

And the storm comes: the whole horizon of sea approaches in a single wave under an oppressing sky; has leapt the breakwaters, hurled sandy spume at circular colonnades, at porticoes, seaweed is on the benches, driven almost to window-grilles, to flowerbeds where huge cinerary urns of dead seasons, vanished games, steps on wooded paths, rise on pilasters; berryblack clusters of water are incandescent violet—copper lids hung on walls respond, glass cupboard-fronts, and unsuspected cracks, fractures, flaking, decrepitude, appear on the walls, now enormous udders lean on the mountains, trunks of fleeing elephants, on mountains' spines, on crests, in hidden sources of valleys and torrents, earth's veins and arteries swell.

Then the suburban street becomes livid with mud, littered with snapped twigs and branches, and will not see the herdsman outlined against sunset as his sheep pass—cloaks steam at cave fires—and the Ave Maria will seek in vain the red and violet bands crossed by black strokes of bird-flights.

And the candles burn and nothing is lost yet, they spread half-tones and parchment-pale gleams, an intimate bedside look on everything, and falterings as when sleep is about to draw the curtain on the world—then only the lamp is the gentle threshold that hides its marrow in wavering rings, is the catwalk that composes interrupted renewals, alters snares in the *maquis,* fallings through trapdoors, terrors of corners in the clearing's breath, dread of the half-open strawrick, in the airy fir where the moon's bells play.

But this anguish, this anxiety?

Hanno messo una coltre su la gabbia degli uccelli e gli usci
esterni sussultano contro vento.

E nulla è perduto ancora;
ma qualcuno ha detto una volta
che un giorno tutto sarà perduto.

They have covered the birdcage and the outside shutters
leap against the wind.
And nothing is lost yet;
but somebody once said
all will be lost one day.

Topazio Affumicato

Guardiamo la pietra di questo anello contornata
di minutissimi diamanti dagli atri riflessi, ed
emerge subito il giorno in cui il fumo basso
a bande, a strisce, a brandelli,
fa d'ogni strada, di tutta la città un solo
cantiere fuligginoso;
in fondo alle vie sembrano oscillare, alzarsi
le gru
e schiume giallicce si spezzano alle stanze
da le pareti di vetro
su le propaggini portuali.
Ed il giorno ha un segreto—è lui che dà un
impercettibile movimento di reticenza alle
labbra e qualcosa che scorre negli occhi rapidissima;
quando passiamo sono aperte le finestre nella
casa dai riquadri di pietra bigia, vediamo
le carte da parato, i gigli di tristi dorature
che non seppero mai primavera.
Ma nelle stanze dai soffitti troppo alti vane
le precauzioni, dei portali,
la perpetua veglia bianca delle cortine,
l'invadenza del colore fumoso non ha ostacoli
avanza, sembra fondersi
sui conciliaboli dei portafiori opachi
nei saloni dove è sospesa, ancora respira
la serata futile, striata di sinistro,

Smoky Topaz

Let us look at the stone in this ring, surrounded
by tiny diamonds with black reflections, and
suddenly the day emerges in which low-hanging smoke
in bands, strips, tatters,
makes of every street, of the whole city
one big sooty dockyard;
at the far ends of streets
cranes
seem to sway, lift,
and yellowish foam breaks on the
glass-walled rooms
on the harbor's ramifications.
And the day has a secret—it is she who imparts
a slight sign of reticence to the lips
and something which flickers briefly
in the eyes;
when we pass the windows are open
in the house of gray stone blocks, we see
the wallpaper, sad gilded lilies
that never knew spring.
But in rooms with too-lofty ceilings, vain
the precautions of portals,
the perpetual white vigil of curtains,
the invasion of the smoky color meets no obstacles,
seems to dissolve
on the conventicles of opaque flower-stands
in the salons where futile evening

—e l'argento dei manici era brunito, e l'oro
soffocato fra gli smorti velluti.
S'erano consumate le lampade alla specchiera,
nella ricerca di quella acconciatura di capelli
vista nel disegno, inafferrabile, sfumata
—due plumelie infine, stanche si lasciarono
cadere sul marmo.
E paziente, ostinata, la mano traeva innanzi
spingeva indietro i buccoli, con l'ausilio
della forcina dall'interno rigonfiava le ciocche
prendeva i fili uno ad uno
perché tutto sembrasse vapore, cinerino di leggerezza, senza
                                                    contorni,
come quando col dito, nel disegno, si stemperano
i tratti del carbonello.
Ma del giorno, del suo segreto, dell'acconciatura
non restano che i riflessi di questa gemma in
crespo che pensa alti ombrati soffitti,
e la litografia sul coperchio d'una scatola di cartone.—

hangs, still breathes, streaked with disaster—
and the silver of handles was tarnished, the gold
smothered among lifeless velvets.
The lamps on the dressing-table were burnt out,
in the search for that coiffure
seen in the drawing, unattainable, faded—
at last two plumelia-blossoms, weary, let themselves
fall onto the marble.
And patient, stubborn, the hand drew forward
pushed back curls, with the help
of a hairpin puffed out locks of hair from the inside,
took the strands one by one
so that all seemed vapor, weightless ash,
without outlines,
as when with your finger, in a drawing, you blur
the strokes of charcoal.
But of the day, of its secret, of the coiffure
nothing remains save the reflections of this gem
in crepe that broods about high shadowed ceilings,
and the lithograph on the cover of a cardboard box.—

Ronda

Nell'ore a capo chino, nell'ore
perdute, a volte d'intorno
si libra ronzando, ci sfiora
la ronda di sillabe mute,
gli scarabei della favola! accenni
di labiali, di sibilanti senza
vocali, impalpabili impronte
di voci negate anelanti
a una cellula d'aria che vibra;
messaggi degli erebi vani
che in noi scava il tempo, svanite
crisalidi d'aspettazioni
discese senza ritorni
che forse un barlume rimuove
da un labirinto di giorni,
in bilico su minimi vortici
di silenzio, o sospese ad un filo
di senso, hanno la misura
dell'attimo di sabbia che scende . . .
poi dispaiono, le riprende
un'altra ronda piú scura.

Patrol

In the downcast, the lost
hours, at times the patrol
of mute syllables hovers around,
buzzing, grazing us,
fabled scarabs! hints
of labials, of sibilants without
vowels, impalpable imprints
of denied voices gasping
for a cell of vibrating air;
messages of the empty hells
time hollows in us, vanished
chrysalids of expectations
descents without return
which perhaps a faint gleam displaces
from a labyrinth of days,
teetering above tiny vortices
of silence, or hung from a thread
of sense, they are the size
of the moment of sand that falls . . .
then they disappear; another darker
patrol recaptures them.

I Giorni

I giorni della luce fragile, i giorni
che restarono presi ad uno scrollo
fresco di rami, a un incontro d'acque,
e la corrente li portò lontano,
di là dagli orizzonti, oltre il ricordo,
—la speranza era suono d'ogni voce,
e la cercammo
in dolci cavità di valli, in fonti—
oh non li richiamare, non li muovere,
anche il soffio piú timido è violenza
che li frastorna, lascia
che posino nei limbi, è molto
se qualche falda d'oro ne traluce
o scende a un raggio su la trasparente
essenza che li tiene—
ma d'improvviso nell'oblio, sul buio
fondo ove le nostre ore discendono
leggero e immenso un subito risveglio
trascorrerà di palpiti di sole
sui muschi, su zampilli
che il vento frange, e sono
oltre le strade, oltre i ritorni ancora
i giorni della luce fragile, i giorni . . .

The Days

The days of fragile light, days
caught in a fresh
tossing of branches, a meeting of waters;
the current carried them far off,
beyond horizon or remembering—
hope sounded in every voice
and we searched for them
in the gentle hollows of valleys, in springs—
oh don't call them back, don't disturb them
even the most timid breath
does them violence;
leave them in limbo; it is enough
if gold gleams from a fold
or slides down a ray onto the transparent
essence that contains them—
but all at once in oblivion, in the dark
depths where our years decline,
a sudden great luminous awakening
will pass with the sun's pulsings
over mosses, water jets
the wind shatters, and they are
beyond streets, beyond returning,
the days of fragile light, the days . . .

Ombre

Le sognanti, lontane ombre che sono
dietro le tue parole questa notte,
fantastiche o dolenti le portava
la corrente dei giorni, il vento che apre
i colori, ed ognuna il suo segreto
di dolore o di gioia che il destino
segnò e il buio chiude;
e ancora altre ne chiami
che dileguando diedero un'impronta
di lume: la promessa d'un ritorno;
mani che schiusero i riposi,
occhi che riflettevano i meriggi
sotto i rami, le foglie della vite
che il raggio fa vivaci, oh le stormenti
stagioni attorno ai volti, l'ore
che scendevano a noi come in dolcezza
umana fatte miti da uno sguardo:
viva siepe, riparo che fa
sicure in cerchio notti, albe, tramonti,
e come pianamente
rispondevano ad ogni sole
che mai le avrebbe, mai sfiorate il rombo
del mistero; ma in fondo ad ogni svolta
è il dolore, la cenere che tocchi
si riga: brace e sangue.
E sul quadrante gira un segno:

Shadows

The dreaming distant shadows
behind your words tonight,
fantastic or grieving, were borne
here by the days' current, the wind that opens
colors, and each with its secret
of grief or joy which destiny
stamped and dark encloses;
and you evoke still others
which dissolving left an imprint
of light: promise of return;
hands that unfolded repose,
eyes that reflected noons
under boughs, vine leaves
a ray quickens—rustling
seasons around faces, hours
that descended to us with a human
sweetness gentled by a glance:
live hedge, refuge that makes nights,
dawns, sunsets, safe within a circle,
and how softly
they responded to each sun,
the rhombus of the mystery that never would
have touched them; but at the bottom of every turn
is sorrow, the ash you touch
is streaked: embers and blood.
And a sign moves on the quadrant:

indietro lascia la vacua spirale
dove l'anima è presa, e fuori attorno
ferma è la notte come una memoria
di sempre; su lo spiano
pietroso che sovrasta al mare basse
macchie di luna e cespi,
tarde stuoie di nuvole, ed un'ansia
s'alza, d'ignoto, ricade: respiro
dell'aria scorre tra le gole, tocca
la paglia sotto il ponte, a le pareti
della cava risale e sovra i margini
si cela tra le fronde degli ulivi.

leaves behind the empty spiral
in which the soul is meshed, and all around outside
night is still as a memory
of forever; on the stony
plain that overhangs the sea
low patches of moon and tufts,
slow cloud-mats, and anxiety
of the unknown rises, falls back: a breath
of air flows between gorges, touches
the straw under the bridge, climbs
to the quarry walls, and above its brink
hides among olive-fronds.

CANTI BAROCCHI E
ALTRE LIRICHE

BAROQUE SONGS AND
OTHER LYRICS

Canti Barocchi

Baroque Songs

Oratorio di Valverde

Ferma il volo Aurora opulenta
di frutto, di fiore,
balzata da rive vicine
diffondi ancora tremore
di conchiglie, di luci marine,
e le valli dove passasti alla danza
pastorale fra le ginestre
t'empirono le canestre
di folta, di verde abbondanza
—a larghe onde di campane tessuta
venivi, dai fili di memorie, dai risvegli infantili—

Traevi con te ne l'incanto
le migrabonde stagioni,
ognuna ora dona il suo vanto
e sono albicocche in festoni,
pesche, ciliege, viticci attorti,
orgoglio fragrante degli orti.

Gracile Primavera cui biancospino
punge il piede errante nel cammino
èsita, implora, non osa
turbare nel sonno la rosa.
Poi labbro che soffia seme di fuoco
la ridesta a poco a poco,
e l'Estate la coglie, la spande
in ampie volanti ghirlande.

82

Oratorio for Valverde

Cease your flight Aurora opulent
with fruit, with flower,
sprung from nearby banks,
spread again tremor
of seashells, of marine lights,
and the valleys where you changed to pastoral
dance among the broom
filled your baskets
with thronging green abundance—
in broad waves of bells you came
woven from strands of memories, from childish awakenings—

In the enchantment you drew with you
the migrant seasons,
each hour flaunts its boast
and there are festoons of apricots,
peaches, cherries, twining tendrils,
the orchards' fragrant pride.

Graceful Spring whose hawthorn
pricks the foot wandering on its way
hesitates, implores, does not dare
disturb the sleeping rose.
Then lips that blow seed of fire
reawaken her little by little,
and Summer seizes her, scatters her
in wide flying garlands.

83

E Autunno, Inverno che dona?
Inverno per le notti all'altare
globi di gocciole gelate tra ginepri
che la luce fa turbinare,
e i venti quando l'organo rintrona.

Fra le volute, fra gli archi che vincono gli estri
piú snelli delle tastiere, pavoni, uccelli del paradiso, fagiani
bevono in conche cilestri,
la fuggitiva dell'Arca porta l'oliva
fra i melograni.
Su le mensole accanto ai messali gravati
di cuojo gli antifonarî (hanno stuoli
di rondini su occasi affocati):
schiuderanno i voli alle tortore del canto
negli albi cieli pasquali;
non muove l'Anno su cardini di firmamento
né per vie di pianeti
ma lo volge dolce e lento
cerchio di melodie.

(Ai quattro punti del Mondo
muovono Arcangeli il vento e i colori)
—ma già nel tempo
spirò dall'occidente un soffio insonne
e accende di cannelle, di cinnamomi,
di rostri porporini i cammini dell'aure
di malie d'arbusti le chiome dei venti i transiti marini.
Di là dalle Colonne
si stende la piana di spume di crespe abbaglianti,
s'erge nei fondali la mole di pomice mora,

And Autumn, Winter, what do they give?
Winter through nights at the altar
globes of frozen drops among junipers
that the light sets spinning
and the winds when the organ thunders.

Among whorls, among arches that outdo
the nimblest fantasies of the keyboards, peacocks, birds of
                                    paradise, pheasants
drink from pale blue shells,
the fugitive from the Ark bears the olive
among pomegranates.
On corbels next to missals weighted
by leather the antiphonals (which display flocks
of swifts on flaming sunsets)
will unfold flights to the turtle-doves of song
in white paschal skies;
the Year does not move on hinges of firmament
nor through the planets' paths
but a circle of melodies turns it
soft and slow.

(At the four corners of the World
Archangels move the wind and the colors)—
but already in time
a sleepless breath of air blew from the west
and it ignites with canella, cinnamon,
with rosy beaks the breezes' course,
with magic spells of shrubs the winds' manes, the sea ways.
Beyond the Pillars
extends the plain of foam of dazzling ripples,
the mass of black pumice rises in the ocean deeps,

s'alzano i re dai manti di piume
nei vortici del sole.

    ...oltre le volte vicino ai campanili
    ove la mano dell'Evangelista
    alta indice alle nubi il volo,
    bianco attonito di cellette, di ballatoi,
    d'intonaco nudo riflette
    tutto l'aereo sospeso mattino.

Ma dove spirano raggiere ed ombre muschiate
all'interne gallerie, alle grate delle tribune
(trascorrono lucerne la notte)
ove vanto di forme gonfia ringhiere tralci campanule soffia
                                         dorate
s'affollano spicchi di volti fra garze consunti profili di lune.
*

*Andavano già lontane
in grande lagrima d'aria
che luce segreta diffonde
e muovon da l'alto campane
in gloria, profonde.*

*Altre: nel pallore che langue e che sogna
segnati i destini sotto la dolorante
trama di vene e di sangue.
Ma chi sa i cammini
dell'anima solitaria?*

*Piegarono a la corrente
d'onde volubili, d'aria,*

86

kings with feather cloaks rise
in the vortexes of the sun.
>   . . . beyond the vaults near the bell-towers
>   where the Evangelist's hand, high up,
>   directs the flight of clouds,
>   astonished white of small cells, landings,
>   of bare plaster reflects
>   the whole airy suspended morning.

But where gleams and musky shadows breathe
in interior galleries, railings of the tribune
(oil-lamps pass at night)
where vaunt of forms swells balconies, tendrils, blows gilded
>   bellflowers
crescents of faces throng among gauze, worn profiles of
>   moons.

*

They were already far off
in a great weeping of air
that scatters secret light
and from above bells, deep-voiced, move
in glory.

Others: in the pallor that languishes and dreams
destinies are stamped under the aching
weft of veins and blood.
But who knows the ways
of the solitary spirit?

They bent to the current
of fickle waves, of air,

al denso fogliame ove il serpente
nell'ore incerte soffia la voce,
                                                Signore
dove è spirito? dove è senso?

L'intrico su l'anima grava
dal tempo antico d'Adamo;
e fragile è l'anima: risuona
e si frange ed ogni giorno abbandona
ai chiodi, al martello le palme,
e non tormento di Sette
Dolori che schiuse pace infinita,

ma il vento che piange ed il fiele
celato a l'ambigua corolla;
e sembra che veli
i calici l'ombra sinistra
e più tenace s'appigli
il fuoco nel germoglio al fiorire . . .
la raffica scuote, il virgulto travia;

da l'alte spire
dei cieli vermigli, Maria,
non splenda raggio né piova fiore
di paradiso, ma scenda
sopore di primi giorni,
su l'erbe in ombra
fresco d'albe remote.

to the thick foliage where the serpent
whispers his words,
     Lord
where is spirit? where is sense?

The tangle weighs heavy on the soul
since the ancient days of Adam;
and the soul is brittle: it rings
and shatters and abandons every day
to the nails, to the hammer the palms,
and not the torment of the Seven
Sorrows that revealed infinite peace,

but the wind that cries and the gall
concealed in the ambiguous corolla;
and it seems the sinister shadow
veils the chalices,
the fire takes hold more tenaciously
in the flowering bud . . .
the squall buffets, the young shoot strays;

from the high convolutions
of vermilion skies, Mary,
let no ray shine, no flower
of paradise rain, but let
the torpor of the first days descend
onto the shadowed grass
coolness of remote dawns.

La Meridiana

Guarda l'acqua inesplicabile:
contrafforte, torre, soglio
di granito, piuma, ramo, ala, pupilla
tutto spezza, scioglie, immilla;
nell'ansiosa flessione
quello ch'era pietra, massa di bastione,
è gorgo fatuo che passa, trillo d'iride, gorgoglio
e dilegua con la foglia avventurosa;
sogna spazi, e dove giunge lucente e molle
non è che un infinito frangersi di gocce efimere, di bolle.
Guarda l'acqua inesplicabile:
al suo tocco l'Universo è labile.
E quando hai spento la lampada ed ogni
pensiero nell'ombra senza peso affonda,
la senti che scorre leggera e profonda
e canta dietro ai tuoi sogni.

Nell'ora colma, nelle strade meridiane
(ov'è l'ombra, ai mascheroni anneriti
alle gronde scuote l'erbe l'aria marina)
rispondono le fontane,
dalla corte vicina (lasciò la notte ai muri
umidi incrostazioni di sali, costellazioni
che il raggio disperde),
dai giardini pensili ove s'àncora il verde
si librano cristallini archi
s'incontrano nell'aria incantata alle piazze

The Sundial

Regard water the undecipherable:
            buttress, tower, granite
throne, feather, branch, wing, pupil,
it fragments, dissolves everything, multiplies it a thousand-
                                                    fold;
            in the restless bending
what was stone, bastion's bulk,
        is an empty whirlpool that passes, a ringing rainbow,
                                    a gurgle,
and vanishes with the adventurous leaf;
it dreams spaces, and where it reaches shining and soft
is nothing but an endless bursting of ephemeral drops, of
                                                    bubbles.
            Regard water the undecipherable:
                at its touch the universe wavers.
And when you have turned out the lamp and every
thought sinks weightless in the dark,
you hear it running light and deep
and singing behind your dreams.

  At the full hour, in streets of noon
(where there is shade, in blackened masks
in gutters sea air stirs the grass)
the fountains answer
from the neighboring courtyard (night left incrustations
of salts on the damp walls, constellations

sui cavalli di spuma gelata,
s'alzano volte di suono radiante
che frange un istante e ricrea
—la tenera piovra, il fiore liquido emerge, elude
il silenzio e un àndito schiude fra il canto e il sopore;
s'aprono zone di solitudini, di trasparenze,
e il bordone poggiato al sedile riposa
e il sogno si leva . . .

L'ombra del cavalcavia
batte al selciato che brucia.

Ora piana ora ferma, ti guardi, ti specchi beata
in alta murata di loggia—nitore di vela—in altana
e la loggia, la cupola, la cuspide che vuole
salire piú alta, sono immerse nel vento del sole;
permea l'azzurro le travature corrose,
la scala che sale alla cella, delle aperture
dei muri forati, degli archi fa sguardi sereni,
e le cavalcature riposano ai fieni falciati;
rigoglio di lantane, di muse, di calle,
ai terrapieni ove il gelso arpeggia l'ombre
ed alle balaustre scendono diffuse
le molli frane
del caprifoglio,
(dietro il cancello fra gli aranci
l'acqua nascosta ha note d'uccello)

E le montagne, le montagne l'han consumate al corale dei
raggi

which a ray dispels),
from hanging gardens where greenness anchors,
crystalline arches balance,
meet in the piazzas' enchanted air
on the horses of frozen foam;
vaults rise of radiant sound
that breaks and recreates an instant—
the tender octopus, the liquid flower emerge, elude
the silence and a hallway yawns between song and

somnolence:

zones of solitude open, transparencies,
and the pilgrim's staff rests propped against the bench,
the dream takes wing. . . .

The shadow of the overpass
beats on the burning flagstones.

Now flat, now still, you look at yourself, you are beatified
on the high loggia-wall—clearcut sail—in the belvedere
and loggia, cupola, the pediment that wants to
climb higher, are immersed in the sun's wind;
blue permeates rotting roofbeams, the stair
that climbs to the cell, gazes calmly through
apertures in the riddled walls, through arches,
and the saddle-horses rest in the scythed hay;
exuberance of lantana, bananas, calla lilies,
on terraces where the mulberry tree
plays on the shadows like a harp,
and the soft landslides
of the honeysuckle
fall, diffused, onto balustrades,

le rèsine, l'erbe odorose, gli aromi selvaggi.
... lancia il sole crinale cerchio
nell'idrie ove l'acqua scintilla,
e s'uno scende l'altro sale,
—armonica d'oro—
la Bilancia appena oscilla
quasi uguale.

Attendono i vegliardi;
sotto la cupola al segno rotondo
(in gemini) folgora l'ora eco di cosmi,
ed alle siepi del mondo
passa il brivido di fulgore
fende l'immane distesa celeste,
vibra, smuore, tace,
vento senza presa e silenzio.

Ma se il fugace è sgomento
l'eterno è terrore.

(behind the gate among the orange-trees
hidden water sounds birdnotes).

And the mountains, the mountains have been consumed at
the rays' chorale
by resins, scented grasses, wild aromas . . .
the sun tosses circles of hair
in the water-jars where water flashes
and if one falls the other rises—
golden harmonics—
Libra scarcely fluctuates,
almost balanced.

The venerable old men wait;
under the dome with the spherical sign
(in Gemini) gleams the hour, an echo of universes,
and a shivering splendor passes over
the world's barriers,
splits the huge stretch of heaven,
vibrates, pales, is still,
wind without grasp, and silence.

But if the fleeting is dismay
forever is terror.

Scirocco

E sovra i monti, lontano sugli orizzonti
è lunga striscia color zafferano:
irrompe la torma moresca dei venti,
d'assalto prende le porte grandi
gli osservatori sui tetti di smalto,
batte alle facciate da mezzogiorno,
agita cortine scarlatte, pennoni sanguigni, aquiloni,
schiarite apre azzurre, cupole, forme sognate,
i pergolati scuote, le tegole vive
ove acqua di sorgive posa in orci iridati,
polloni brucia, di virgulti fa sterpi,
in tromba cangia androni,
piomba su le crescenze incerte
dei giardini, ghermisce le foglie deserte
e i gelsomini puerili—poi vien piú mite
batte tamburini; fiocchi, nastri . . .

Ma quando ad occidente chiude l'ale
d'incendio il selvaggio pontificale
e l'ultima gora rossa si sfalda
d'ogni lato sale la notte calda in agguato.

Sirocco

And over the mountains, far above horizons
a long strip of saffron:
the moorish wind-swarm breaks through,
takes the main portals by force
the lookout-turrets on the enamel roofs,
batters façades from the south,
tosses scarlet hangings, blood-red pennants, kites,
opens blue clearings, cupolas, dream-forms,
jolts pergolas, vivid roof-tiles
where spring-water stands in opalescent jars,
scorches suckers, makes twigs of shoots,
turns hallways to trumpets,
plummets onto faltering garden growth,
snatches forlorn leaves
and young jasmine—then, grown milder,
taps tambourines; bows, ribbons. . . .

But when the wild pontifical
folds in the west its wing of fire
and the last red pond flakes off
on all sides hot night rises in ambush.

La Notte

La notte si fa dolce talvolta,
se dalla cerchia oscura
dei monti non leva alito di frescura
perché non sòffochi, ai muri vicini apre corimbo di canti,
sale coi rampicanti pei lunghi archi,
    alle terrazze alte, ai pergolati, al traforo
dei mobili rami segna garofani d'oro,
segreti fievoli coglie ai fili d'acqua sui greti
o muove i passi stanchi
dove l'onde buje si frangono ai moli bianchi.

Subito allo schermo dei sogni
soffia in vene vive volti già cenere, parole àfone . . .
muove la girandola d'ombre:
sulla soglia, in alto, ognidove
vacuo vano, andito grande tende a forme,
sguardo che muove le prende,
sguardo che ferma le annulla.

Riverberi d'echi, frantumi, memorie insaziate,
riflusso di vita svanita che trabocca
dall'urna del Tempo, la nemica clessidra che spezza,
è bocca d'aria che cerca bacio, ira,
è mano di vento che vuole carezza.

Alle scale di pietra, al gradino di lavagna,

Night

If the cool breath that keeps
us from stifling does not lift
from the mountains' dark circle,
sometimes night turns tender,
unfolds a cluster of songs on the walls nearby,
mounts with the creepers through long arches
      to high trellised terraces, pergolas; reveals
gold carnations in the moving branches' fretwork,
gathers dim secrets from threads of water
on the river's gravel, or takes tired steps
where dark waves dash themselves against white wharfs.

Suddenly on the screen of dreams
it breathes alive faces long since ash, soundless words . . .
it turns the weathercock of shadows:
on the threshold, above, everywhere,
a void, a great corridor leads to shapes
a quick glance catches,
a fixed stare annihilates.

Reverberations of echoes, shards, unsatisfied memories;
backwash of vanished life that overflows
time's urn, the hostile sand-glass that shatters,
is air's mouth seeking a kiss, anger,
is wind's hand desiring a caress.

On stone stairs, slate steps,

alla porta che si fende per secchezza
è solo lume l'olio quieto;
spento il rigore dei versetti a poco a poco
il buio è piú denso—sembra riposo ma è febbre;
l'ombra pende al segreto
battere d'un immenso
Cuore
    di
       fuoco.

at the door splitting from dryness,
the only light is quiet oil;
little by little the versicles' rigor is spent,
darkness thickens—seems repose but is fever.
The shadow hangs from the secret
beating of an immense
Heart
     of
       fire.

Bosco il Prestigiatore

"*Stridere di carriola che porta fronde morte
vogliamo che sia gola di cristallo sul ramo;
e delle vane querele del nostro cuore inquieto
vogliamo fare segreto di stelle e di fontane.*"

Bosco the Conjurer

*"We wish the creaking of the barrow that carries
dead branches were a crystal throat on the bough,
and our unquiet heart's vain litigations
a secret of stars and fountains."*

Al Tempo di Re Borbone

Giorni erano quelli, e poco bastava perché fiorisse
il racconto, la favola, e il labbro era pronto,
l'orecchio era attento fra i volti sospesi,
la parola era spiga al vento
spessa di grani che sparge l'aria
a la città perplessa, al borgo sonnolento,
ai casolari lontani.
Girava l'arcolaio dell'ore tempi di pacata attesa
di freschi ritorni ai vasti divani di tela fiorata.
Erano salvezza nella tempesta marina
i fuochi di Sant'Elmo e l'Orsa serena
tornava a brillare in punta di piedi sul mare,
innanzi ai fari, innanzi all'altalena
buia della costa vicina.
*

Terrore a la riva: la furia dei ratti
trae fra gli strilli la gonna come bandiera
e il corsaro dagli occhi di nera porcellana,
da la barba serpentina:
la scimitarra stride con l'arma paesana,
il fortilizio in collera a mezzo il colle
e da ringhiera o pertugio di muro
la bombarda spaccona in salti di fuoco che tuona
come tamburo su palco di fiera.
Poi sembra che porti il tumulto
piú grande, la calmeria:

104

At the Time of the Bourbon King

What times those were, a little was enough to make
story and tale flower, and lips were ready,
ear attentive among expectant faces,
the word was a wheat-spike in the wind
thick with grains the air scatters
to the confused city, the sleepy town,
to distant farmhouses.
The hours' skein-winder spun times of quiet waiting,
of fresh returns to vast divans of flowered linen.
St. Elmo's fire was salvation in the tempest
and the serene Bear
returned to shine on tiptoe on the sea,
before the lighthouses, before the dark
seesaw of the nearby coast.
*

Terror on the strand: fury of abductions
drags the skirt like a banner among shrieks
and the corsair with black porcelain eyes
and snaky beard;
scimitar clashes with rustic arms,
halfway up the hill the angry fortress
and from the parapet or an opening in the wall
the braggart mortar in spasms of fire that thunders
like a drum on a fairground stage.
Later the dead calm
seems to bring greater tumult:

l'acqua che irriga spande la sera
negli orti.

irrigation water spreads evening
in kitchen-gardens.

L'Ammonimento

Ma fra le quinte è apparso chiromante, indovino:
"in figure d'enigma chiudi le tue venture,
con l'ombra aspidi alati volano ne la ramaglia,
stridulo scherno scuote l'infida boscaglia;
ma tu la porta un poco socchiudi e guarda i veli
delle piogge lontane;
getta nel braciere corteccia di pino,
al davanzale appendi ciuffo di rosmarino,
e una lampada accendi al tuo silenzio celato:
verrà nei sogni oro filato di cieli,
e nella chiusa stanza, nel calmo splendore
vedrai svanire il mondo
nel volto rotondo d'un fiore."

The Warning

But from the wings a palmist, fortuneteller:
"Lock your future in enigmatic figures:—
with shadows asps fly into lopped branches;
strident mocking jolts the malign undergrowth.
But you—leave the door ajar and watch veils
of distant rains;
throw pinebark into the brazier,
hang a clump of rosemary on the windowsill,
and light a lamp to your hidden silence.
Sky's spun gold will come in dreams
and in the closed room, in calm splendor,
you will see the world dissolve
in a flower's round face."

Il Prestigiatore

"Negli inverni translucidi, nella reggia dalle grandi gradinate che scendono verso la riviera di conteria celeste, una sera di spettacolo, egli alzò la pistola, tirò il colpo a lo specchio, e lo stagno verticale sembrò balzare in frantumi sul palchetto, sconvolse gli archi aciduli, i flauti dai lagni pastorali, i contrabassi ventruti . . . Ma poi fu distesa la neve d'un lino su la vitrea rovina e, tolta, l'acqua tornata serena, rifletté di nuovo dalla portiera dell'aula immensa, in fondo, le uniformi nane e impettite, le costellazioni dei candelabri alteri.

"L'ora sembrava indugiare incerta nel fuoco dei pendagli, s'irrigidiva dinanzi ai pendoli sentenziosi, si piegava alla danza, di zebre cristalline, di giraffe che l'orchestra disegnava nette, negli arti sottili, sugli spazi inesistenti. Ma ecco, ch'egli viene, e ognuno vede che l'ora non è trascorsa, egli l'ha tenuta in mano delicata, come una farfalla d'oro, l'ha fermata, infissa ad uno spillo, su la falda del suo vestito . . ."

Seguite adesso un poco quello che dirò:
Pensate ch'io abbia davanti una tavola da disegno e in essa la scena sia già pronta im ombre forti, in luci rare. È la strada di uno di quei sobborghi che circondano la città di calmi rumori, di caseggiati bassi, e immaginate che tutto cominci ad oscurarsi: fra poco un'ora di notte soffocherà quel che rimane ancora dei colori precipitati dal tramonto; fumi vagabondi, improvvisi fasci di luce rossastra in getto, interrotti dalla porta che sbatte. La poca luce se l'è presa tutta il torrente scarso d'acqua che serpeggia fra mulini di-

The Conjurer

"In the translucent winters, in the royal palace with the great staircases that descend toward the coast of blue glass, one evening performance, he raised the pistol, fired at the mirror, and the vertical pond seemed to leap in splinters onto the stage-box, upset the acidulous bows, the flutes with their pastoral laments, the big-bellied double-basses. . . . But then flaxen snow was spread on the ruined glass and, removed, the water turned tranquil, reflected again from the portiere at the back of the vast hall, the dwarf stiff uniforms, the constellations of the haughty candelabras.

"The hour seemed to linger, irresolute, in the pendants' fire, tautened before sententious pendulums, yielded to the dance of crystalline zebras, giraffes clearly designed by the orchestra, in subtle arts, on non-existent spaces. But look—he comes, and everyone sees that the hour has not passed, he has held it in his delicate hand, like a gold butterfly, has fixed it, pierced by a pin, to the edge of his frock-coat. . . ."

Now follow for a while what I am about to relate:

Imagine that I have a drawing-table in front of me, and on it the stage is already set in deep shadow, few lights. It is a street in one of those suburbs that surround the city with quiet sounds, with low house-blocks; and imagine that everything is beginning to darken: very soon an hour of night will suffocate what still remains of the colors precipitated by sunset; vagrant smoke, sudden shafts of reddish light darting, interrupted by the door banging. The scant light has all been swallowed up by the meager stream that winds between

rotti, fra canneti spani, dove fra le gore macera lo straccio, ormeggia il galeone d'una zucca, giú giú fino all'orizzonte marino, su cui ha un riflesso ancora del giorno trasmigrato la spola gialla d'una nuvola.

Ora con la mia matita disegno un viaggiatore e, poi lascio che si muova da solo: va col passo di chi viene da lontano, un passo in cui vedi l'ombra della piroetta, l'inchino cortigiano, sale i gradini d'arenaria d'una bettola, vuole bervi un bicchiere prima dell'ingresso nella città vicina. Getta sopra una panca il ferraiolo che sente i cavalli da posta. Sul tavolaccio di rugoso olivo è interrotto lo scambio delle carte per l'ospite insolito, posano le rotondità delle coppe, le sagome unte delle regine senza dolcezza. Nell'aria è la presenza invisibile delle nasse aride, delle alghe disseccate, dei picconi, e il lavoro del giorno si stempera ora nelle giacche ammucchiate.

Ma non potreste immaginare quel che il viaggiatore farà ora, con un sorriso sibillino: prenderà le carte le piegherà un poco perché possano stare dritte, e postele in fila cosí, s'irrigiderà poi in una posa di comando ed al suo gesto meccanico ecco che andranno avanti l'una dopo l'altra come allo scatto di una invisibile molla, sul tavolo, poi balzando da questo sul mattonato, sul davanzale, via nelle notte . . . —e il tavolo, la finestra, i volti, le mura sembrano sorgere, bruciarsi e continuamente risorgere nel crepitio leggero di una candela, come una vibrante lanterna magica; e lo stupore arrotonda le bocche o le inarca, fa che le braccia pendano, nel nativo atteggiamento dell'uomo senza aggettivi dinanzi all'ignoto.

ruined mills, between canebrakes with stripped roots, where a rag steeps among mill-races, the squash-galleon moors down, far down, all the way to the marine horizon, on which the yellow shuttle of a cloud still holds a reflection of transmigrated day.

Now with my pencil I sketch a traveler, then let him move by himself: he walks with the gait of one who comes from afar, a gait in which you see the shadow of the pirouette, the courtly bow; he climbs the sandstone steps of a tavern, wishes to drink a glass there before entering the nearby city. On a bench he tosses down the heavy cloak which smells of posthorses. On the large table of furrowed olive-wood the card game is interrupted for the strange guest. They set down the goblets' rotundities, the greasy profiles of sour queens. The invisible presence of dry creels is in the air, desiccated seaweed, pickaxes, and the day's work dissolves now in the pile of jackets.

But you could never imagine what the traveler is going to do now, with a sybilline smile: he will take the cards, bend them a little so they can stand up straight, and having placed them like that, in a row, will then stiffen himself in an attitude of command, and at his mechanical gesture, look: they will go forth one after the other as though at the jerk of an invisible spring, on the table, bounding thence onto the brick floor, onto the windowsill, away into the night—and table, window, faces, walls seem to rise, burn, and continually resurge in the light crackling of a candle, like a vibrating magic lantern; and astonishment rounds mouths or arches them, makes arms hang, in the natural gesture of the man devoid of adjectives confronted with the unknown.

Le Carte in Cammino

Fila di carte in cammino,
sotto il cielo a tutte l'ore,
respiro d'una favola ti manda
dove palpita ancora: la notturna
locanda ora t'accoglie, sotto i tetti
fumidi o dove al torbido lumino
passa lo zoccolare dei muletti,
il coro dei sonagli colora d'argento
—nasconde il basto il fiore e l'oro—
T'accolgon le vallette esigue
quando la frescura cala
e cigola la passerella
sui fusi dell'acque turbinanti
e sovra comignoli, sovra vette
di montagne, di cipressi, di pioppi
nel distacco fumoso fra la
notte ed il giorno luce oscura
una pendula luna d'almanacco.

e i giorni mutano volto
e muta volto la vita
i quadranti dicono i segni
degli impossibili ricorsi
nell'eterna dipartita.

Va la piccola compagnia

Cards on the March

Row of cards on the march
beneath the sky at all hours,
breath of a fable sends you
where it still pulsates: the nocturnal
inn now welcomes you, under smoky
roofs or where in dim night-light
the clopping of mules passes,
the chorus of silver-sounding harness bells—
flower and gold hide the packsaddle—
slender valleys welcome you
when coolness falls,
over spindles of eddying water
the footbridge creaks,
and above chimneys, above the tops
of mountains, cypresses, poplars,
in the smoky separation between
night and day, a pendulous
almanac moon gleams faintly.

and the days change face
life changes face
quadrants tell the signs
of impossible recurrences
in eternal departure.

The small company passes

sotto il cielo violetto che già
pensa i giorni dell'uva matura,
ed ogni pensiero, ogni voce,
ha dolcezza di ritorni;
passano lontano, per tramonti,
per albe, l'ha visti il mandriano
che veglia, i pastori al fuoco
ne lo scuro passare, quando
Fioravante mena la spada
con l'ombre sul muro.
Salgono colline, scendono valli,
i cavalli dormono sotto i ponti,
talora stanche le regine
riposano nei fienili;
ai re le coppe degli assi,
coi vini tracannati
spengono i rimpianti, delusi
dei regni mai regnati,
delle futili corone;
e nelle soste l'asso di bastone
pianta il suo palo fiorito
in mezzo ai chiusi degli ovili.

mistero d'ogni minuto:
entra il vento da le fessure,
ma non l'hai sentito, ha mosso
d'un leggero trasalimento
nell'armadio socchiuso il vestito

Errano sotto la tunica leggera

under the violet sky which is already
contemplating days of the ripe grape,
and each thought, each voice,
bears the sweetness of returns;
they pass far off, through sunsets,
dawns, the herdsman who
stands guard, the shepherds by the fire
have seen them pass in the dark, when
Fioravante* brandishes a sword
with the shadows on the wall.
They climb hills, descend valleys,
the horses sleep under bridges,
sometimes the tired queens
rest in haylofts;
with gulped wine
the aces' goblets blot out the regrets
of the kings, disappointed
by kingdoms over which they never reigned,
by their futile crowns;
and in the pauses the ace of clubs
plants his flowering staff
in the middle of the sheepfolds' enclosures.

mystery of every minute
the wind enters through the cracks
but you did not hear it, it moved
the garment in the half-closed wardrobe
with a slight tremor.

They wander under the flimsy tunic of

* a familiar figure in Sicilian puppet-shows

de la pioggia di Primavera
—ha visto i pallidi colori
chi prende sopore nella penombra—
Ascendono i capi,
a l'erme specole dove
i messaggi dei pianeti
in fosforiche frange
guizzano a le pareti:
—pendolo, ruota, sestante,
vertigini di culminazioni:
ne la spelonca stellare
è in breve segno la marea che leva
la conca verdebruna
del fantastico mare.

vanno al grande respiro
le chiome dei platani, degli ulivi
e la rete dell'ombre sui banchi
vuol chiudere i fantasmi dell'ore
che non sono, che non saranno:
i giorni sono stanchi
sebbene i rami in fiore.

Spring rain—
the twilight sleeper
has seen the pale colors—
The leaders climb
to lonely observatories where
the planets' messages
flicker in phosphoric fringes
on the walls:
pendulum, wheel, sextant,
vertigo of culminations:
in the starry cave
a short sign marks the tide that lifts
the greenbrown shell
of the fantastic sea.

the tresses of plane trees, of olives
move with the great breath
and the shadows' net on benches
seeks to enclose phantasms of the hours
that don't exist and never will:
the days are weary
for all that branches are in flower.

L'Anima e i Prestigi

Ma l'anima confondono i prestigi:
intimidita abbassa la scriminitura
che parte le nere chiome, le palpebre ombrate;
nel cestello ripone la matassa,
gli aghi, il ditale, piega la fioritura
paziente sul bianco, nelle sere.
E la lontana dimora di nuovo l'accoglie:
serbano le scansie tenebrose
pallide ampolle, o, pendenti
in vimini dal soffitto,
e un poco oscillano quando
passa la tramontana; spirare
senti con l'erbe della solitudine, l'altura.
A la tarda ora solo guarda l'alto
abbaino la stella polare.

The Soul and Sleights of Hand

But sleights of hand confound the soul:
intimidated she lowers the parting
that divides black hair, shadowed lids;
in the sewing-basket she puts away skein,
needles, thimble, patiently folds
flowering on white in the evenings.
And the distant dwelling receives her again:
murky shelves hold
pale cruets, or, suspended
in wicker baskets from the ceiling,
they sway slightly when
the *tramontana* passes; you smell
uplands breathe with the grass of solitude.
At this late hour only the polar star
watches the high attic-window.

Sebbene Tu Cerchi

Sebbene tu cerchi che la tua stessa
fugacità sia l'arpa, il flauto, il ruscello,
sai che su la fronte è il segno
di una malinconia senza fine;
e se l'aria della notte che avanza
scioglie la maggiorana, i mirti,
il chiaro calice della datura
in fumo umido di fragranza,
sai che la favola sboccia,
poco dura, s'allontana,
e l'amaro è dell'ultima goccia.
Anche se il disperso ritrova
il confine, il lume notturno, il riposo,
anche se il tumulto gioioso
delle campane irrompe
nell'aria della sera,
e la corona da le gemme invernali
dolce si curva a la Primavera dei bianchi sponsali.
Ora su le colline oscure, su le curve dei monti
le terse cinture, le cacce di scintille
prende il primo scoramento che poi trascolora,
e saranno in fondo a le valli, brusio, brina,
all'eriche sonaglio di stille che vapora,
breve fluire di fonti che l'erba disperde,
che la terra densa ai raggi caldi beve.

Although You Seek

Although you seek to liken your own
fleetingness to the harp, the flute, the brook,
you know your brow bears the mark
of endless melancholy;
and if the air of advancing night
looses marjoram, myrtles,
the datura's clear chalice
in a damp smoke of fragrance,
you know the story unfolds,
lasts briefly, moves off,
and the last drop is bitterness.
Even if the lost recovers
its confines, night-light, resting place,
even if bells' glad clangor
erupts in evening air,
and the crown of wintry gems
curves gently to Spring's white nuptials.
Now on dark hills, on sweeps of mountains,
clear bands, chasing of sparks;
the first deep dejection that later fades sets in
and deep in valleys
there will be a rustling, hoar-frost,
on heather bell-drops that evaporate,
brief flow of springs which the grass disperses
and the earth, heavy with warm rays, drinks.

Liriche

Lyrics

Mobile Universo di Folate

Mobile universo di folate
di raggi, d'ore senza colore, di perenni
transiti, di sfarzo
di nubi: un attimo ed ecco mutate
splendon le forme, ondeggian millenni.
   E l'arco della porta bassa e il gradino liso
di troppi inverni, favola sono nell'improvviso
raggiare del sole di marzo.

Inconstant World

Inconstant world of gusty
rays, pallid hours, of perpetual
flux, cloud-glory:
a moment and see—
changed forms glitter, millennia sway.
And the arch of the low door, steps smooth
with too many winters, are a story in the brusque
brilliance of the March sun.

Dove Spore di Sole

Dove spore di sole
frangono spume in volo
s'aprono all'avventure
vibran spazi marini;
nube corriera allaccia
i promontori e balza
fuga leggera d'echi.
 Ma dove già si ferma
l'ombra ne l'alta veglia
di fusti e di fogliame,
sapienza di sorgive
sospesa l'aria incanta.
 E nell'alture (male
d'erbe la pietra invade)
già buio di cisterna
pensa colori e forme:
nei sonni scenderanno
reclini su l'ignoto.

Where Sun-spores

Where sun-spores
shatter flying foam
open themselves to adventures
marine spaces shake;
a cloud-courier links
the promontories and a light
echo-fugue bounds.
But where shadow already
stands still in the high vigil
of boles and foliage,
suspended awareness of springs
enchants the air.
And in high places (bane
of grass invades the stone)
already the cistern's dark
ponders colors and forms:
in sleep they will descend
recumbent on the unknown.

Si Provano d'Osso le Nocche

Si provano d'osso le nocche
a battere sui tavolati,
penombra d'intorno, fortuna
crescente volubile calca.

E tinge a sanguigna la fiamma
i volti di fusto e di solco
native cortecce, millenni
di monte, di raffiche e sole.

A gesti di vanga e di falce
promettono re senza regno
l'oro di nubi a ponente,
inganni le dame ed i fanti
e il matto canzoni tra i fieni.

E pendono l'ore ed i tralci;
graticci disseccano i doni
dell'anno, confortano l'aria.

Ma fuori altro gioco: (chiudete
finestre, fessure, abbaini)
non luce di lampada evada
non penetri furia di stelle.

Se sbuchi dal vicolo invano
le sfuggi, t'incombono, ai tetti

The Bony Knuckles Try

The bony knuckles try
to rap upon the planks,
half-shadow encompassing, fortune
waxing fickle tramples.

And the flame dyes sanguine
the faces of stump, furrow,
native bark, millenniums
of mountain, of squalls and sun.

At the gestures of spade and scythe
realmless kings promise
the gold of western clouds,
queens and knaves promise deceits
and the joker—songs in the hay.

And hours and tendrils dangle;
trellises dry the year's
gifts, comfort the air.

But outdoors is another game: (close
windows, cracks, skylights)
let no lamplight escape
don't let the fury of the stars penetrate.

If you emerge from the alley, in vain
you flee them, they hang over you, from roofs

sospendono piume spettrali
membrane, veleni di luci
cangianti, losanghe, ventose.

Né vale a riparo covone
di frasca, tepore d'ovile
o legno che bruci sereno:
dardeggia, saetta la stella.

S'alzano conici colli
frane di diafani lumi
sovrastano buie vallate,
in alti profili di rupi
si tengono i casolari
su angusti burroni, la chioma
di folti castagni li sfiora
dispersi nel turbine immoto.

hang ghostly feathers,
membranes, poisons of changing
lights, rhombs, suckers.

Nor do sheaf of branches, warmth
of sheepfold or quietly burning wood
avail as shelter:
the star darts, shoots arrows.

Peaked hills climb,
landslides of diaphanous lights
overhang dark valleys,
on high profiles of cliffs
farmhouses cling
above narrow ravines, the mane
of thick chestnuts grazes them
scattered in the motionless whirlwind.

Di Soste Viviamo

Di soste viviamo; non turbi profondo
cercare, ma scorran le vene,
da quattro punti di mondo
la vita in figure mi viene.
   Non fare che ancora mi colga
l'ebbrezza, ma lascia che l'ora si sciolga
in gocce di calma dolcezza;
e dove era il raggio feroce, ai muri vicini
che celano i passi ed i visi,
solleva una voce improvvisi giardini.

   E il soffio è sereno che muove al traforo
dei rami i paesaggi interrotti
e segna a garofani d'oro
la trama delle mie notti.

We Live by Pauses

We live by pauses; don't let deep searching
trouble you, but let the veins flow,
from the world's four corners
life comes to me in images.
  Don't make intoxication seize me
again, but let the hour melt
in drops of serene sweetness;
and where the fierce ray was, on walls
close by that hide footsteps and faces,
a voice summons up unexpected gardens.

Air's breath is serene that stirs fractured
landscapes in the branches' fretwork
and marks with gold carnations
my nights' weft.

Veneris Venefica Agrestis

Sorge dalla macchia terragna, il volto
—ilare, arcigno—stretto nel nero fazzoletto
sembra di castagna risecchita, il capello
che ne sfugge non è vello gentile
ma riccio caprigno; quando va
(non sai se ritta o china) il bruno piede contratto
è ràdica che d'un tratto sbuca dalla terra e cammina.

    Bada che non t'offra la tazza di scorza
dove l'acqua è saporosa di radici, di foglia vischiosa,
o la mora, o la sorba, il frutto silvestre che lusinga
le labbra ma lega la lingua.

    Governa, sembra, la forza
delle lune crescenti
che gonfia le cortecce e alterna
gl'invincibili fermenti
i flussi, le linfe . . .

    Pronuba come gli uccelli
che portano i semi lontani
reca gli innesti arcani.

    Ed i muri terrosi del casolare crollante
ove l'ortica ha lo stelo gigante
sono i suoi regni ombrosi,
accende i primi legni nei forni favolosi.

    Ed i fumi che salgon davanti
alla porta o dagli orti vicini
sono i mobili turbanti dei suoi vespri sibillini.

Veneris Venefica Agrestis

She rises from low scrub, her face—
merry, stern—bound in a black kerchief
seems of dried chestnut, the hair escaping
is not soft fleece but
goat-kink; when she passes
(upright or stooped, you can't tell) her gnarled brown foot
is a root that suddenly breaks from the ground and walks.
   Take care she doesn't offer you the bark-cup
where the water is pungent with roots, sticky with leaves,
blackberry, or sorb-apple, the wild fruit that flatters
lips but binds the tongue.
   She rules, it seems, the force
of waxing moons
that swells bark and alternates
the invincible ferments
floodtides, sap. . . .
   Pronubial as the birds
that carry distant seeds
she brings arcane graftings.
   And the muddy walls of the crumbling farmhouse
where the nettle lifts its giant stalk
are her shadowy realms,
she lights the first wood in fabulous ovens.
   And the smoke that rises before
the door or from gardens nearby
is coiled turbans of her sybilline vespers.

137

Scolopendra la sanno le tenebre
di morte norie fra il capelvenere.
  È la maschera che accenna e dispare
quando fanno voraci l'ombre interne
i lucignoli semispenti appesi
alle moliture notturne, ai palmenti,
e sono nell'aria sentori d'ulive pigiate
d'accesi vapori di mosti, e vengono le lanterne
bilanciate ai passi delle calzature chiodate.
  Complici delle sue trame sono i gesti
delle fatiche agresti:
curvarsi a cogliere le foglie secche, le ghiande . . .
e la movenza misurata sui piedi scalzi
quando è grande fastello su le teste
e non vedi fronte, né ulive d'occhi,
ma solo la bocca vive . . .
fascia la veste i fianchi, il busto, ed ha
grazia—la frasca passando lascia
odore di siccità . . .
o il gesto che alza la brocca
rinata dalla vasca.
  Curva segna il cerchio:
al suo cenno sale
dalla terra tremenda
la corrente primordiale;
(e il piede che preme il solco irrigato
e la mano che impugna la vanga
ora chiama possente altra brama)
forte si fa dei fiati dei chiusi
dei richiami diffusi, delle lettiere

The darkness of dead irrigation-wheels
among maidenhair knows her as poisonous centipede.
   She is the mask that beckons and disappears
when surrounding shadows make voracious
the half-spent wicks hung
from nocturnal grindings, from millstones,
and the air is heavy with hints of pressed olives
of kindled must-fumes, and lanterns balance to
the tread of nailed boots.
   Partners in her plots are the movements
of rustic toil:
the stooping to gather dried leaves, acorns . . .
and the measured barefoot gait
when a great faggot-truss weighs the head
and you do not see brow or olive eyes,
but only the lively mouth . . .
the dress wraps hips, waist, and is
full of grace—the passing branch leaves behind
the scent of dryness . . .
oh the gesture that lifts the reborn
pitcher from the basin.
   Bent, she marks the circle:
at her signal
the primordial current
rises, tremendous, from the earth;
(and the foot that tramples the irrigated furrow
and the hand that, powerful, grips the mattock
now evokes another longing)
she draws strength from the breaths of sheepfolds
from diffuse cries, from the animals' damp steaming

umide e brucenti, dei sarmenti affumicati,
e l'ombra ove senti le bardature di sacco e di corda,
i canestri bagnati, ove dalla soglia scorgi
la mola inerme, le marre use al piglio rurale,
rustica lievita l'ombra di voglia ancestrale.
I cisti i cardi le pulicarie le nepitelle
che sembrano aromatiche e fresche
sono se non ti guardi l'esche
d'una spirale che tutto piega,
(intacca la notte bianco metallo
senza lega di raggio siderale)
inquina financo la curva della dolce collina.
Ora è nel giorno, una mano alla quercia,
l'altra pendente—suadente e lercia,
nera come scopa di forno la veste . . .
e la folata improvvisa a la scarpata
scioglie e inonda di celeste
intrico di foglie, di fronda.
Pure promette, dischiude l'ardore
la freschezza, il vigore del respiro
che solleva la pesca, l'amara dolcezza
del fiore di mandorlo; sotto la fronda rude:
sbocci carnosi violenti selvaggi germogli,
fra i lunghi ventagli delle felci
messaggi ambigui di funghi,
sguardi incerti d'acque fra i trifogli,
e un senso di nude crete primigenie
presenti, vicine
dove il pioppo desta arsura, sete
con miraggi stormenti di rivi

140

bedstraw, from smoky brushwood,
and the shadow where you smell harnesses of sacking and
rope,
soaked baskets, where from the threshold you perceive
the defenseless millstone, hoes inured to the rural grip;
rustic, the shade of ancestral desire ferments.

   Rockroses thistles plantains catmint
which seem aromatic and fresh
are, if you don't watch out, snares
of a spiral that enfolds everything,
(night eats into the unalloyed white
metal of the sidereal ray)
corrupts even the curve of the gentle hill.

   Now she is in daylight, one hand on the oak,
the other dangling—persuasive and filthy,
her dress black as an oven-broom . . .
and the sudden gust of wind on the escarpment
frees and floods with blue
a tangle of leaves and foliage.

   Yet she promises, discloses the ardor,
the freshness, the vigor of the breath
that lifts the peach, the bittersweetness
of the almond-blossom; under the rough foliage:
fleshy buds, violent wild sprouts,
among long fans of ferns
ambiguous messages of fungi,
wavering glances of water among the trefoil,
and a sense of naked primordial clay
present, nearby
where the poplar awakens raging thirst
with mirages of streams rustling

e specchio si fa d'ogni aura che muove,
dove sott'ombra di monte
i ripidi declivi
la valletta si fa stretta
e si chiude
in bocca di fonte
fra muschi sensitivi.
   Se la nuvola un poco si posa
sul ciglione o su la soglia
della valle, nell'ombra viva
ora vede timone d'aratro
che scuote che sfiora che sfoglia
il cespo e la rosa boschiva.

and makes itself a mirror of every breeze that stirs,
where beneath the mountain's shadow
the steep declivities
the valley narrows
and closes itself
in the spring's mouth
among sensitive mosses.
    If the cloud rests for a while
on the brow or on the threshold
of the valley, in the living shade
now she sees the ploughshaft
that shakes skims strips
tuft and sylvan rose.

La Luna Porta il Mese

La luna porta il mese
e il mese porta il gelsomino,
spenge salendo la luna
contese di forme lontano e vicino.
Pesca la fronda della palma
nell'azzurro. L'Orsa
si cela in lenti lini lunari;
oggi è lago di calma
e domani non è dolore.
Guarda come pende da la grata
il fiore del geranio, come splende il lumino
e tante stuoie distese;
la luna porta il mese
e il mese porta il gelsomino.
Salgono al belvedere
occhi che fanno fresca
l'oscurità, son luci vane
riflessi del fanale che trema
alle pareti vibranti ancora
del tremito delle campane?
È l'aria che l'alto aspira
e sale frusciando le scale?
Ma sopra alle ringhiere
piega appena il vento velo
o nuvola, il belvedere
tocca l'Orsa che annega
nel gorgo lontano del cielo.

The Moon Brings the Month

The moon brings the month
and the month brings jasmine;
the rising moon blurs
opposing forms, far and near.
A palm-frond fishes
in azure. The Bear
hides in loose lunar flax;
today is a calm lake
and tomorrow holds no grief.
Look how the geranium hangs
from the grating, how the night-lamp shines
on stretched matting;
the moon brings the month
and the month brings jasmine.
Eyes which freshen darkness
lift to the belvedere;
are the lights
empty reflections of the lantern
which shakes on walls still vibrating
to the bells' beating?
And is it air that aspires to the heights
and goes up staircases, rustling?
But above the balustrade
wind sail or cloud scarcely
bends; the belvedere
touches the Bear which drowns
in sky's distant abyss.

Se vuoi gustare il sapore
della sera, a gocce di fonti
empi una tersa brocca
senza spezie, aromi, od erba
e un poco alta la tieni:
verranno col sorso alla bocca
l'ombre, il respiro dei monti
e il colore che l'acqua serba.
Scivolan l'ore sospese,
pesci in globo cristallino,
la luna porta il mese
e il mese porta il gelsomino.

If you want to taste
evening, fill a clear pitcher
with drops from springs,
free of spices, aromatics, or herbs,
and hold it up, not too high:
with each sip, shadows,
mountain-breath and the color
water keeps, fill your mouth.
Suspended hours slip by,
fish in a crystal globe.
The moon brings the month
and the month brings jasmine.

Lunghi Tralci

Lunghi tralci, lunghi tralci mi strinsero
mi chiusero braccia;
specchiavo conca notturna
d'acque montane, sapevo
le radici e le fonti, alla bruma
leggera passavano l'ombre
dei giorni, sorgevano i volti
fra la speranza e il dolore;
ed era tepore primevo
ritorno e infinita carezza.
Ma quando il risveglio
m'apre i mattini e mi posa
su le sponde della luce
reco un balsamo ignoto
un olio che mi fa dolci
le cose, in silenzio consuma,
e mi ridona il mondo
in risonanze, in memorie
(e indugiano i giorni in lenti
meriggi, in vesperi immensi).
Cosí vado fra gli echi le nuvole e i raggi.
non m'è straniera la spiga
della lavanda che brucia l'aria
o il petalo bianco ai cespugli
furtivi di vento.
Dietro le colline respira

Long Tendrils

Long tendrils, long tendrils bound me,
pinioned my arms;
I mirrored the nocturnal shell
of mountain waters, knew
roots and sources,
into fine mist
days' shadows passed, faces
loomed between hope and despair;
and primeval warmth was
return and infinite embrace.
But when waking
opens mornings to me and sets me
on the borders of light
I bring an unknown balm
an oil that mellows things
is consumed in silence,
and gives me back the world
in resonances, memories
(days linger in slow
noons, vast evenings).
So I go among echoes clouds and rays,
no stranger to me the spike
of lavender that scorches air
or the white petal in the thickets
furtive with wind.
Behind the hills the season

la stagione, scendono i declivi,
ed è cosí molle il cammino
sui viali dove le svolte
spengono l'ansia dei passi
che gli orizzonti fra i rami
svaniscono, sorgono ancora,
in abbandono di spazio.
Lunghi tralci, lunghi tralci mi strinsero,
mi chiusero braccia
ed era ritorno, promessa;
ma nella luce, nel giorno
ove inclino l'ore al canto
e va l'acqua fievole nella creta che brucia
serbo l'ombra serbo la malia:
mai tace il colloquio nascosto,
mai posa la voce segreta.

breathes, slopes plunge,
and the way through avenues
where turns blot out
fear of footsteps
is so gentle that horizons
disappear among branches,
reëmerge in abandonment of space.
Long tendrils, long tendrils bound me,
pinioned my arms
and it was return, promise;
but in the light, in the day
where I incline hours to song
and water trickles in burning clay
I keep the shade, I keep the sorcery:
the hidden colloquy never stills,
the secret voice never settles.

Ma Nella Notte che Varca

Ma nella notte che varca
—e fila silenzio ai borri
e macera stelle ne le
insenature raccolte—
invano cercherai fermare
col tuo calamo d'oro
sulle fluide cortine
il tulipano che non muta!
Si perderà fra i rigidi
cipressi e le querce
incontro al fragile stellato,
sarà fatuo ghirigoro,
melodia che palpita
solo del suo dileguarsi;
e l'ansia, i dardi,
le implorazioni del canto
si spengeranno a soglie
infinite a labili arcobaleni
e la lampada che ti dà
nimbo e sembra che arda
di piume in luce, di chiome
accese guarda come
tacita avventa alle pareti
l'ombre, come le tormenta
per poco d'aria che muove . . .
riconosci i terrori di una volta?

But in the Night That Crosses

But in the night that crosses,
and spins silence to gullies
steeps stars in
huddled inlets
you will seek in vain to pin
the changeless tulip
to fluid curtains
with your gold quill!
It will be lost among taut
cypresses and oaks
against brittle starlight,
will be a scrawl without meaning,
a melody that pulses
only in the dying;
the anguish, darts,
song's supplications,
will die away to countless thresholds
to shifting rainbows,
and the lamp that gives you
a halo seems to burn
with feathers of light, manes
on fire, see how, silent,
it casts shadows on the walls,
how air's slightest current
torments them . . .
do you recognize the old terrors?

Ma forse lo splendore
d'ogni giorno è la gemma
che manca a la corona
quando il tempo, bianca
lacrima, svanirà, e se ancora
l'anno muoverà la zona
multicolore delle stagioni
sempre saranno la muta
bellezza e il dolore che implora.

But perhaps each day's
splendor is the gem
missing from the crown
when time, a white tear,
will vanish, and if the year
still moves the multicolor
belt of seasons
there will always be mute
beauty and importunate grief.

Caccia

Il cielo ha qualche banda lilla
nel fermo azzurro; su piana, su creste,
scoppia smargiasso lo sparo:
a rimbalzo poi si allontana
in giravolte fra colli, fra rocce,
si spenge in erto burrone di sasso;
ma piumaggio sanguigno non piomba,
solo viene alle nari
l'amaro di polveri arse,
di fondelli bruciati
fuso al selvatico delle ginestre,
all'umido delle crete;
ripete lo sparo
alza fusto di fumo
che accenna passeggera ombrella;
ma la caccia non s'arrende e il cacciatore
meno che prende più s'arrovella:
vibra d'estrema ansia il cane,
il piede s'apre il sentiero fra gli spessi
cespi, invade frondosi recessi
dove il giorno è larva verde che trema,
oscilla il passo, cade,
fra le selci taglienti e le rupi.
Ora è la volta
della ruvida frasca vicina:
fruga il bracco, la pietra lanciata casca,

The Hunt

Sky's steady blue is lilac-
streaked; on plains, on peaks
the braggart shot explodes:
fades away, rebounding
in twists among hills, rocks,
dies in a stony ravine;
but no bloody plumage plummets,
only the bitterness of scorched powder
burnt cartridges
reaches the nostrils
merged with wildness of the broom,
clay's damp;
the shot repeats
a shaft of smoke rises,
suggests a passing parasol;
but the quarry doesn't yield and the less
the hunter bags the more incensed he gets;
his dog shivers with extreme anxiety,
foot opens a path through thick
clumps, invades leafy recesses
where day is a tremulous green ghost,
the step wavers, falls
among cutting flints and boulders.
Now comes the turn
of the rough branch nearby:
the hound searches, the hurled stone falls,

ma non balza la selvaggina,
non si parte la freccia di piume!
Solo il lume eguale del sole
e l'aria a filo di lontananza
portano la fiumara, il promontorio, la marina,
e l'alterna risonanza dell'onda;
(talvolta all'avvento di prime nuvole
scorre lesta ombra per piani, per valli,
nulla: una lepre di vento).
E tu ghiandaia ribatti
secca la beffa silvestre,
e scatti l'arida nota
l'aria ferma percuota!
Il richiamo poi rimbalzi
in trama d'echi
di vallette in vallette,
di ramo in ramo
in capitomboli, salti, fischi;
ma rispondono dagli alti
verdi eremi: piú dolce
cade la goccia della campanella
—e incrina specchi celati di cerchi, di righe,
—ruotano gli orologi, suonano l'ore del bosco,
e ne le nicchie crespe d'aria
        scuotono le collane d'argento.
Da le cattedre di fogliame
commento dell'ironico uccellame:
hanno occhiaia sapiente, austeri becchi,
pulpiti, leggii, stecchi, grucce, trampoli, didattiche bacchette;
ma il piffero volatile si spezza

but no game-bird breaks cover,
no feathered dart takes flight!
Only the even sunlight
and air on a thread of distance
bring torrent, promontory, seashore,
and the alternating sonority of the wave;
(sometimes at the onset of first clouds
a swift shadow runs through plains, valleys,
nothing: a wind-hare).
And you jay confute
the sylvan mockery
and loose the dry note.
Strike the still air!
Let your call ricochet
in a weave of echoes
from valley to valley
branch to branch
in headlong tumbles, leaps, whistles;
but they answer from high
green retreats: the bellflower's
bead drops more gently
and cracks hidden mirrors with circles, lines;
clocks revolve, the woods' hours strike,
and in niches ripples of air
               shake silver collars.
From leafy rostrums
commentary of the ironic bird-realm:
they have knowing eyes, austere beaks,
pulpits, lecterns, twigs, perches, stilts, didactic rods;
but the winged fife breaks

dove giunco verdeggia a le sorgenti.
E poi rete di bosco prende il cielo
e fin che spira tutto lo frastaglia:
mobili schegge a querce, orli a cipressi,
i rami dondolanti al soffio, i tralci
fioriscono d'aeree pervinche,
liquido stagna dove avvalla, dove
folto viluppo, edera, boschiva
alga, polipo in fronde stringe azzurro,
soffoca cielo.
Ma il sole già flette
piú dolci i raggi
e il volto del giorno piega alla sera;
nell'aria àtona, molto in su passa
la schiera in lacca scura
delle nostalgiche gru.
E passano le sagome stanche
nei colori del ritorno, stampa
il passo su le smorte sabbie,
prende il viottolo che sale.
Non empire di canti fulminati,
        di voli infranti la carniera,
guarda la storia,
        che lasciò nera sull'intonaco la lucerna,
e il mazzo delle pere
        che allo stipite la paglia aggancia,
disseta il mucchio delle mele
        ch'hanno i tramonti sulla guancia,
—e sono appagati i sogni
d'olio scarso, splendono i giardini

where a rush greens at springs.
And then a net of woods catches sky
and as long as the breeze blows slashes it to shreds:
moving oak-splinters, cypress edges,
branches swaying at a breath of air,
the airy periwinkles' tendrils flower,
liquid stagnates where it sinks, where
a dense tangle (ivy, wood algae,
polyp in fronds) binds azure,
chokes sky.
But the sun already slants
its rays more softly
and day's face folds to evening;
in toneless air high above,
black-lacquered, the file
of nostalgic cranes crosses.
And the tired shapes pass
in the colors of return, the step
imprints pallid sands,
takes the small path that climbs.
Don't stuff the game-bag with shattered
                songs, broken flights,
look at history,
                that left the oil-lamp black against plaster,
and the bunch of pears
                which straw binds to the doorpost,
the heap of apples, thirst-quenching,
                with sunset on their cheeks;
then dreams are satisfied
with scarce oil, phosphorescent

fosforici, vengono i riposi costellati
al veleggio di celesti astri marini,
e dove finiscono i sentieri
accenderà l'inverno le serre luminose:
d'immense felci l'esili nervature, in trasparenza
il sottobosco, i muschi, i ciclamini.
Dopo tanta speranza spenta consola
la vuota carniera nella stanza che sa di terriccio
vicino alla brocca la sola
foglia di menta, di rosmarino, di alloro!
Si estenuano le vite in cacce fallite,
la mano pura disegna
sulla pioggia che passa: illusione.
Ma fiorirà il bastone
del mendicante che attende
la sua misura d'olio,
e poi scende nella pianura
alla sua notte dai paraventi,
dai cuscini di foglie,
da le maschere moventi ai rami,
dai pioppi sui torrenti
arsi nei lampi d'oro.

gardens glow, starred rest
comes with the sailing of marine constellations,
and where paths end
winter will kindle luminous greenhouses,
fine veins of enormous ferns,
transparent undergrowth, mosses, cyclamens.
After so much spent hope,
in the room which smells of humus,
the single leaf of mint, rosemary, laurel near the pitcher
is consolation for the empty game-bag.
Lives wear out in fruitless hunts,
the pure hand sketches
on passing rain: illusion.
But the staff will flower
of that beggar who waits
for his ration of oil
and then descends into the open plain
to his night of screens,
leaf-cushions,
masks moving among branches,
poplars above parched
stream-beds in gold flashes.

PLUMELIA

PLUMELIA
for Antonio Pizzuto

Guida per Salire al Monte

Così prendi il cammino del monte: quando non
sia giornata che tiri tramontana ai naviganti,
ma dall'opposta banda dove i monti s'oscurano in gola
e sono venendo il tempo le pasque di granato e d'argento
—al cantico d'ogni anno s'avvolge di bianco la crescenza,
trabocca dai recinti, l'acquata nuova ravviva
la conca, l'orizzonte respira—da lì
alito non soverchio di vento di mezzogiorno,
e allato ti sarà e ti farà leggero
compagno che non vedi, presente
per una foglia che rotola o un ramo che oscilla,
e sono i sandali il curvarsi dell'erbe innanzi . . . canna
non avrai né fiasca di zucca per la sete come
al tempo delle figure, dal vento nascono i sogni. Ancora
un indugio tiene l'estate, di dalie, di gravi
campanule troppo accese ai giardini bagnati,
guai se l'aria l'agiti un poco!
e vengono afflati di vane danze—ma
la risacca indolente nelle insenature
cullò già rottami sperduti di mesi,
è questo il tempo, prendi il cammino del monte
e non discordi il passo nella salita al soffio
tacito—se i rami svolta agli arbusti
rassembrano pendenti piume di tortore di beccacce.
Spiazzo dinnanzi e un fonte, e questo è l'imbocco
della salita, scalea montana che poggia

Guide for Climbing the Mountain

So take the mountain road: provided
it is not a day when the *tramontana* blows against sailors,
but from the opposite side where mountain gorges darken
and the time of garnet and silver Easters draws near—
at each year's canticle growing things wrap themselves in
white,

overflow surrounding walls, the new shower revives
the basin, the horizon breathes—from there
a slight gust, not too much, of noon wind
which will be beside you, will be a gentle
unseen companion, present
in a leaf that spins, a bough that sways,
and the curving of the grass before you is your sandals...
you will have neither cane nor gourd-flask for your thirst
as in the time of images, dreams born of the wind.
Summer still lingers, with dahlias, heavy
Canterbury bells too inflamed in drenched gardens;
beware if the air shakes them even slightly!
and breaths of futile dances arrive—but
the inlets' lazy backwash
has already rocked the lost flotsam of months,
this is the time, take the mountain road
and don't let your footstep clash on the ascent with the silent
breath of air (if it turns the branches on the bushes,
they resemble dangling feathers of turtle-doves, of
woodcocks.)
A clearing before you and a spring, and this is the entrance

su arcate giganti in muraglia coeva
alla rupe e stipano i vani siepaglie
densissime di sterpi serpigni, rifugio
nell'ore della luce di quanto la notte
ronfa, erra, sfiora—l'acciottolato rurale
fa scivoloso il piede, chè ogni pietra circonda
il muschio ora verde ora arsiccio,
ai margini il muretto a secco sgretola
e sul pietrisco punge il cardo violetto . . . ma guarda
sopra l'altura, è vicina, non la tocchi con mano?
Pure se vi affiorano nuvole a ricci a corimbi
—spume che nel celeste muovono i venti dell'alto—
subito si discosta la vetta, t'incombono sopra le nubi.
Silvestri le prime rampe, quando svolti alla terza
intorno t'è l'aria del monte come non altrove:
un liquore di fiori rupestri, d'antiche piogge e segreti,
e vedi calcare che un giorno immemoriale una stecca
segnò come creta a incavi sottili, a mensole, a nicchie,
e incontri già la capanna dell'eremita:
edicola o cella? senza copertura o riparo
squallida d'inverni, agli schianti
quì che il monte s'interna, di levante o scirocco,
lontano pareva di vimini, di carta—
pesta dipinta—s'asconde o vien fuori secondo
ch'è nuvolo o secco il solitario? L'eremita
chi lo vide mai? E noi pensiamo mattini
boschivi, anime di cortecce, veglie . . . ma così non è.
Forse crano suoi enigmi di schioppo e lanterna,
forse era lui a cercare nella forra angusta
il bulbo che alimenta la notte?

168

to the climb, mountainous stair that rests
on giant arcades in a high wall coeval
with the rock, and thick overgrown hedges
of snaky twigs crowd the empty spaces, refuge
in daylight hours of whatever
snores, wanders, skims by at night—the rural cobbles
are slippery underfoot, for moss now
green now parched encircles every stone,
the dry stone wall crumbles at the edges
and on the rubble the violet thistle pricks . . . but look
above the heights, it's close, can't you touch it with your
                                                hand?

Even if clouds appear there in scrolls, clusters—
foam which the lofty winds move in the blue—
suddenly the summit retreats, the clouds weigh upon you.
The first ramps are wild; when you turn to the third
the mountain air is around you as nowhere else:
a liqueur of wildflowers, ancient rains and secrets,
and you see limestone which a stick one immemorial day
scored like clay in shallow holes, shelves, niches,
and already you encounter the hermit's hut:
shrine or cell? without covering or protection
bleak with winters, at the blasts
of *levante* and *scirocco*, here where the mountain is cleft—
from afar it seemed made of wicker, of painted cardboard—
does the solitary one hide or come out
according to whether it is cloudy or fine? Who
ever saw the hermit? And we think of woodland
mornings, souls of bark, vigils . . . but it is not so.
Perhaps the enigmas of gun and lantern were his, perhaps
it was he who searched in the narrow ravine
for the bulb that night nourishes?—

—Solitudine trasparenza d'abisso?—
E le notti, le notti hanno un tarlo rovente
né giova scongiuro, le pietre della capanna
serbano ancora le losanghe scure che lascia
fuggendo il rosso devastatore dal manto . . . e questo
avvenne una volta: nell'ora
che su la città è una coltre in caligini,
e scende, né la ferma spranga o chiavistello,
e posa a ognuno la sabbia del sonno su le palpebre,
da un'intacca della rupe sprizzò la scintilla:
saio barba cappuccio, il fagotto d'orbace e stoppa
fu tutto ruote di fuoco sbocchi di fumo . . . l'ombre
dell'energumeno su le pareti di roccia
come di notturni avvoltoi in turbinio d'ali!
Piú delle fiamme paurose . . . tardi dal mucchio
si partirono in volo dintorno maligne
pirauste, lampiri—e dalla pianura
di giù se alcuno vide il bagliore
pensò forse: accende il capraio a conforto
la fiammata, ora che autunno avanza . . .

Solitude, transparency of abyss?—
And the nights, the nights contain a burning worm,
nor does exorcism avail, the stones of the hut
still retain the dark diamond-shapes which
the red devastator drops from his cape as he flees . . . and this
is what happened once: in the hour
when a blanket of mist settles on the city—
neither cross-bar nor bolt can stop it—
and it drops sleep-sand on everyone's eyelids,
from a notch in the rock a spark leapt:
habit, beard, cowl, the bundle of coarse cloth and tow
were all wheels of fire, mouths of smoke . . . the shadows
of the possessed on rock walls
like nocturnal vultures in a turmoil of wings!
More of the terrifying flames . . . later from the heap
malign fire-moths, fireflies took flight on every side—
and from the plain below
if anyone saw the glow he thought, perhaps:
the goatherd is kindling his blaze for comfort
now that autumn draws on. . . .

L'Andito

Scarsa luce di solito ha
l'andito umido: quella
d'uno sportello, pure viene
un giorno e lo raggiunge il sole, e
questo è nell'ore tarde
al tempo dell'anno che i velieri
delle piogge precoci
virano scuri all'orizzonte, brucia
il raggio l'onde e le pianure
e voci di marina e di monte
s'estinguono disperse nel fulgore . . .
Subito fiammei segni
sui muri, accesa
polvere su ciscranne e mensole
d'antico ulivo, e l'ombra del battente
sul pavimento che sente gli inverni
è un'ombra che consuma
memorie e sogni. Solitudine,
e s'alzano i calvari
sconosciuti—pure breve dura:
non serba impronta
della grata di vetro che trascorse
cremisina l'intonaco
della parete, presto
nell'andito è già notte.
E i giorni vanno,
ma se la vita

The Passage

The dank passage
usually gets little light: that
from a small hatch. Yet
a day comes when the sun reaches it;
this is in the late hours
at the time of year when the sailboats
of early rains tack
darkly on the horizon, the ray
burns waves and plains
and voices of sea and mountain
die away, dispersed in the splendor. . . .
Suddenly, flaming signals
on the walls, kindled
dust on armchairs and shelves
of old olivewood, and the shadow of the portal
on the floor that feels winters
is a shadow that consumes
memories and dreams. Solitude
and unknown Calvaries rise up
—but not for long:
it does not retain the imprint
of the glass grille that, crimson,
moved across the plaster
on the wall. All at once
it is night in the passage.
And the days go by,
but if life

dimentica e trasvola
ogni anno in questo tempo
espiatorio il sole
reclino chiama la preghiera,
dell'andito ignorato
fa l'oratorio in fiamme.

forgets and every year
flies quickly in this expiatory
time, the recumbent
sun evokes prayer,
makes of the neglected corridor
a flaming oratory.

Notturno

Hai visto come al varcare la soglia
il lume ch'era nella mano manca
mentre l'altra fa schermo, ha dato uno svampo
leggero dal vetro s'è spento.
Tardo il passo né fu colpo di vento,
forse ha soffiato qualcuno, un volto
subito svaporato nell'aria?
                           Felpata, ovattata
densa di cortine ogni stanza, ogni vano
—solo per la notte che pensa? Imbottiture
a finestre doppie che l'aria non giri
ed anche la porta ha la sua veste
di stoffa che spenga ogni stridio (rinchiuso
interno che la malinconia
di nuovo chiama opprime e la figura
annosa e i fili estremi
incandescenti al flusso giallo).
Non ebbe strisce sanguigne il tramonto,
vennero chiare le campane,
ora pende la lanterna al carretto che stenta
e in fondo alla strada sul mare
un bastimento che prende il largo
gira i suoi fuochi lontani.
E ancora due volte hai riacceso
il lume e due volte s'è spento
all'entrare: una veletta,

Nocturne

You have seen how, crossing the threshold,
the light that was in your left hand,
the other hand acting as a screen,
flickered lightly through the glass and went out.
Your pace was slow, nor was there a lunge of wind;
did someone blow perhaps, a face
that suddenly evaporated into air?
                              Plushed, thickly
padded with curtains every room, every chamber—
only for pensive night? Wadding
on double windows so air does not circulate
and the door too has its mantle
of cloth that muffles every screech (inner
precinct that evokes melancholy
anew, oppresses, the image
full of years and the last threads
incandescent in the yellow floodtide).
There were no blood-red streaks in the sunset,
bells pealed clearly,
now the lantern hangs from the laboring cart
and at the end of the street on the sea
a ship getting under way
revolves its far-off fires.
And twice more you have relit
the lamp and twice it has gone out
as you entered: a veil,

un ventaglio di piume, una mano
che sfilò dal guanto, la falda
d'un portale che non sostenne
il nastro? Ma non c'è nessuno
e sai che non bisogna tentare
il buio: rimemora, ha nostalgie, imprevisti,
l'ombra a le ombre, meglio pregare
a questora, quel che gioco
sembra di giorno fa vero
di notte la notte che sogna—
penso che farai: la luna, i pianeti la rosa
di maestrale o scirocco nei porti
lontani maree: il volume
sibillino di numeri e immagini
che muta in oro innegabile voci
smorzate all'orecchio, significazioni
di sogni, eventi. Ma i morti
non hanno cifre per i nostri tesori,
singulti hanno in noi,
veglie
di fiamme basse, aneliti
d'angoscia verso un nodo di vita
incompreso, e a volte una sera
che scende dall'alto e candori infiniti.
Parlottare fatuo nell'aria
o il buio che si cerca o sfioramenti
di matasse invisibili o altro
certo non saranno che fole,
ma è vero che per tre volte
t'hanno soffiato sul lume al passare.

a feather fan, a hand
that slipped out of the glove, the skirt
of a doorway the ribbon did not
hold up? But no one is there
and you know there is no need to probe
the dark: it remembers, feels nostalgia, the unforeseen,
the shadows' shadow. Better to pray
at this hour; what seems
a game by day
the dreaming night makes true.
I wonder what you will do—the moon, the planets, the
                                                    windrose

of *maestrale* or *scirocco* in
far-off ports, tides; the sibylline
book of numbers and images
that changes muffled voices
to undeniable gold, purports
of dreams, events. But the dead
have no ciphers for our treasures,
they are sobs within us,
vigils
of low flames, anguishings
toward a knot of uncomprehended life,
and at times an evening
that falls and infinite whiteness.
Fatuous babbling in the air
or the darkness that one seeks, or touches
of invisible skeins—surely these will be
nothing but idle tales
though it is true that three times
they have blown on your light in passing.

Il Messaggio Perduto

Richiama le notti nel primo
autunno ancor tiepide e l'aria
ove erra un fermento sperduto
di caprifoglio, avviene che un'ansia
si levi improvvisa ed infranga
l'eguale fluire: tra veglia
e sonno qualcosa è sorta
che sapevamo forse dormendo:
gira fuso, rifolo vano, prendi
corpo di nulla. Si estende
nei chiusi, il bestiame ha sentito
un poco s'agita e il gallo . . . propaga
sul colle dappresso, certo
dalla finestra s'è sporto
un volto tutto solchi d'ulivo
tarlato, piega
la lampada, indaga,
poi scende e su la soglia
riappare il lume, ora è
verso l'asse che i margini giunge
al fosso di macchie e di rupi,
sull'aia s'arresta, dispare—
e ancor più lontano un cane
s'è fatto vivo, batte un uscio
come una botte percossa,—poi cade
di nuovo il silenzio, la notte

The Lost Message

Remember the still-warm nights
of early autumn and the air
where a lost ferment
of honeysuckle strays, it happens that an uneasiness
arises, unexpected, and shatters
the even flow: between waking
and sleep something emerged
that we knew about perhaps while sleeping:
turn, spindle, vacant puff of wind, make
a body out of nothing. It spreads
to the sheepfolds, the animals have sensed it,
they stir a little, as does the cock . . . it spreads
to the nearby hill, surely
a face all furrows
of wormeaten olivewood
leaned out of the window,
the lamp tilts, searches,
then lowers and on the threshold
the light reappears, now it is
toward the plank that joins the banks
of the ditch filled with scrub and rock,
it halts on the threshing-floor, disappears—
and still further off a dog
comes to life, a door bangs
like a struck cask,—then silence
falls again, the night

riprende il gioco di dadi
in cerchi minimi, l'onda
lontana e grave distorce
la fiaccola di prua
al peschereccio. Nel giorno
—dietro i sugheri è un calderone
rovente o un dolce
vapore trai pioppi—nel giorno
verdura non manca nell'orto
non s'è vista impronta
fuggiasca di piede. Nessuno
dirà chi nel tempo del sonno
passò, che messaggio
trascorse ignorato e si sperse.

resumes the game of dice
in the smallest circles, the distant
heavy wave twists
the prow-torch
on the fishing-boat. In daytime—
behind the cork-trees is a red-hot
cauldron or a soft
mist among poplars—in the daytime
there is no greenstuff missing from the kitchen-garden,
no fleeting imprint of a foot
was seen. No one
will say who went by during the time
of sleep, what message
passed, ignored, and was lost.

La Strada Fuori Porta

La strada fuori porta,
e ogni anno agosto
alza fanali d'afa, e accende
la festa sui portali della chiesa
in archi, in pali, le luminarie gialle,
verdi, blu, agita nacchere, trombette
di cartone, dondola barconi
di rosse frutta ferite . . . poi cadono
dai balconi fiori di carta, l'ultimo
palco rimbomba al martello
che lo disfà e a tratti,
già sono le foglie inquiete;
ogni anno fa ritorno
la festa, e la stagione tarda
in zone di svanito rosa,
ai margini del giorno
ferma siepi di bruno viola.
Ma nella chiesa, se scendo
tre gradini, sopra lastre di tombe
dove non giunge l'esitare dei ceri
ognuna ne l'informe
papavero confitta,
vedo l'anime in fuoco:
distorti volti, braccia
levate verso nuvole e colombe . . .
nel profondo

The Street Outside the Gate

The street outside the gate,
and every year August
lifts sultry lamps and kindles
the festival on the church portals
in archways, in poles, the illuminations—yellow,
green, blue—shakes castanets, cardboard
bugles, rocks barges
of bruised red fruit . . . then paper flowers
fall from balconies, the last
scaffold reverberates under the hammer
that dismantles it and at times
the leaves are already restless;
every year the festival
returns, and the season lingers
in areas of faded pink,
fixes brown-violet hedges
on day's margins.
But in the church, if I go down
three steps, above the tomb-slabs
where the tapers' hesitation does not reach
I see souls in the fire,
each fixed
in the shapeless poppy:
distorted faces, arms
raised toward clouds and doves . . .
                              in the depths

del tempo e dei tramonti
lo sguardo si fermò sul fuoco
estremo, poi altrove si volse;
ma dove andava, brune
macchie, seguivano le vespertine
figure di brace e d'angoscia . . .

of time and sunsets
the glance paused at the last
fire, then turned elsewhere;
but where it went, brown
spots, evening figures
of embers and anguish followed. . . .

Le Tre Figure

Se l'aria scende ora più fresca
e più s'accende a ponente
è segno che fra breve tre figure
dietro le grate saliranno
la scaletta che porta alle campane,
alla loggia vicina—un poco
rigide, scure sul tramonto,
guardano attorno,
si piegano su la ringhiera e poi
dispaiono—al saluto
serale di chi s'allontana
batte la porta,
si chiude su le immagini inesauste
della giornata: lo sguardo di chi
traeva la carriola, le chiome
dei platani che fanno largo
alla ventata stanca, le foglie
si sa piegano sempre verso il mare
anche lontano, non visto. Tre
figure e una porta che batte
fanno che se ne vada il giorno,

nero

e rosso, n'è pieno l'occhio,
e girano i paesaggi
dell'ora.

The Three Figures

If cooler air now falls
and the west ignites
it is a sign that shortly three figures
will climb the stairway behind the gratings
that leads to the bells,
to the neighboring loggia—somewhat
rigid, dark against the sunset;
they look about,
lean over the railing then
disappear—at the nightly
greeting of the departing one
the door bangs,
closes on the unexhausted images
of day: the look of the one who
pulled the wheelbarrow, the thick tresses
of the plane-trees that open themselves
to the tired gust of wind; the leaves,
we know, always bend toward the sea
however distant, unseen. Three
figures and a door that bangs
make day vanish,
             black
and red, the eye is filled with it,
and the landscapes of the hour
revolve.

I Sobborghi

In fondo alle strade
dei sobborghi che scendono
verso occidente, il camino
brucia, s'incrociano i tizzi
l'uno fumiga nero, si torce
il bruco arroventato, il cielo sopra
digrada in tenue giallo, verde,
e così nella stanza
dove non hanno ancora acceso i lumi
e opprime il passo spento sui tappeti.

Passò carnevale, nel grezzo telone del cielo
si profilò l'Oca bianca, il lenzuolo
che flette la pertica, immagine
della paura d'un tempo. E le notti?
Tardi quando è sprangato l'uscio
e non più ravviva le faville
alla corrente lo scaldino—mura
strigliate dalla brusca a giallo e blu
contro fermenti di letame, paglia
bagnata e solleone; ora nel buio
altro colore accende.

The Suburbs

At the far end of the suburban
streets that drop
toward the west, the stove
burns, the brands interlace;
one gives off black smoke, the red-hot
caterpillar writhes, the sky above
shades to cold yellow, green;
it is like that in the room
where they have not yet lit the lights
and the footfall lost in the rugs oppresses.

Carnival passed, in the sky's harsh curtain
the white Goose stood out, the sheet
the pole bends, image
of an old fear. And the nights?
Late, when the door is barred
and the brazier no longer stirs
sparks with the draught of air—walls
currycombed by the horse-brush to yellow and blue
against fermenting dung, wet
straw and dog-days; now in the dark
another color catches fire.

I Morti

                        Un'ombra
che s'allungò su la credenza,
o nel cortile sotto la caldaia
l'occhio che ancora luce
quando tutto è spento,
soltanto questo, ma sono
i morti. Male non fanno, che può
un flusso di memoria
senza muscoli o sangue? terrore
dei vani al crepuscolo, bianche
ombre, movenze agli spiani
tesi di luna nei sogni infantili . . .
Pure un turbamento sono, nelle sere
sommesse—pazienza, preghiere.
Sono su le giogaie e i passi
dei monti, anche nei giorni
quando spiegato è calmo il manto
delle domeniche a frange d'oro . . .

The Dead

A shadow
that lengthened on the credenza,
or in the courtyard under the cauldron
the eye that still shines
when everything is extinguished,
only this, but it is
the dead. They do no harm, what power
has a flow of memory
with no muscles or blood? terror
of twilight rooms, white
shadows, movements in extended flat places
of moon in childish dreams. . . .
Still they are disturbing, on subdued
evenings—patience, prayers.
They are on the saddles and the passes
of the mountains, as well as in the days
when the unfurled mantle of
gold-fringed Sundays is still. . . .

Plumelia

L'arbusto che fu salvo dalla guazza
dell'invernata scialba
sul davanzale innanzi al monte
crespo di pini e rupi—più tardi, tempo
d'estate, entra l'aria pastorale
e le rapisce il fresco la creta
grave di fonte—nelle notti
di polvere e calura
ventosa, quando non ha più voce
il canale riverso, smania
la fiamma del fanale
nel carcere di vetro e l'apertura
sconnessa—la plumelia bianca
e avorio, il fiore
serbato a gusci d'uovo su lo stecco,
lascia che lo prenda
furia sitibonda
di raffica cui manca
dono di pioggia,
pure il rovo ebbe le sue piegature
di dolcezza, anche il pruno il suo candore.

Plumelia*

The shrub that was safe from the moisture
of pale winter
on the window-sill in front of the mountain
rippled with pines and rocks—later
in summer-time, the country air enters
and the clayey soil heavy with spring-water
steals its freshness—in the nights
of dust and windy
sultriness, when the inverse canal
no longer has a voice, the street lamp's
flame flickers restlessly
in its glass prison and the unfastened
opening—the white and ivory
plumelia, its blossom
preserved by eggshells on the dry twig,
lets the thirst-parched
fury of a squall
denied the gift of rain
seize it, and even
the briar had its folds
of sweetness, the thorn-bush
a whiteness all its own.

*Inhabitants of Palermo call this shrub *pomelia*, a picturesque distor-
tion, because the flower smells of apple and has the pureness of a
camellia. The plants were once seen on most of the city's balconies.
Winters in Sicily are not severe enough to require their being taken
indoors but the points at which the new blossoms emerge are, or at
least once were, protected by eggshells.

FOR "BAROQUE SONGS AND OTHER LYRICS"

The following is a translation of the afterword written by Eugenio Montale for the first edition of *Baroque songs and other lyrics*.

On April 8, 1954 I received a small book which bore a name unknown to me: Lucio Piccolo. It was enclosed in a yellow envelope, sealed, unfortunately; with a 35-lire stamp. In order to redeem it I had to pay 180 lire more. The book, entitled *9 lyrics*, printed on only one side of the page in worn and barely legible type, bore no inscription but was accompanied by a letter. It stemmed from Capo d'Orlando (Messina), and had been printed by the Stabilimento Progresso-Santa Agata. The typography was no better than that of Dino Campana's *Canti Orfici*, published at Marradi in 1914.

The letter said: "I am taking the liberty of sending you some lyrics of mine which I have had printed privately and do not plan to circulate. In them, especially in the group *Canti barocchi*, about which I feel the most strongly, it was my intent to re-evoke and fix a unique Sicilian world—more precisely that of Palermo—which now finds itself on the verge of disappearing without having had the good fortune to be preserved in any art form. And this, of course, is not because of deliberate choice of a subject but because of an insistent inner need for lyric expression. I mean to speak of that world of baroque churches, of old convents, of souls suited to these places, who spent their lives here without

197

leaving a trace. I have tried not so much to recall as to interpret it from my childhood memories. Read me, and accept my apologies, etc. . . ."

I have written poems, and, what's more, I have written about poets, old and young: which means that every year I receive books of verse by the hundreds. I do not have the flair of Goethe, who, having sniffed the wrapper of a book, would drop it, still unopened, into the wastebasket saying he smelled nothing good in it. I open the books I receive, run through them, and do not even throw them out with the waste paper. They form a pile on my table; every so often a compassionate servant gets rid of it on his own initiative. Lucio Piccolo's book did not form a part of that pile. Maybe I wanted to ascertain whether it was worth 180 lire. I carried it with me, read it absent-mindedly, being rather put off by the letter, which was pretty typical, and of a kind that made me fear purely descriptive poetry. I did not even begin with the baroque poems. I read the first five lyrics, by no means easy or direct, without straining to understand them. I am convinced that poetry is rarely understood in a flash. It is difficult to make the literal sense and the musical sense of a lyric mesh. The two can present various degrees of incompatibility. The rational import may be evident, and the verbal music secret, concealed, almost beyond one's grasp. Or the contrary may happen. On the other hand, a lyric cannot be composed of music alone; it seeks to reveal a meaning which a simple harmony of unintelligible words cannot give it. The distinction between art and poetry that is sometimes evident in the pages of De Sanctis, perhaps not very happily formulated, indicates a need that will probably never be

198

clarified. (The difficulty of making place for poetry next to the so-called arts will always be the stumbling-block of any general, systematic esthetic.)

To close the parenthesis I will say, then, that I read the first poems of the little volume without striving to fix my attention in one or the other of the two directions.

I read:

> Inconstant world of gusty
> rays, pallid hours, of perpetual
> flux, cloud-glory: . . .

And a little further on:

> We live by pauses: don't let deep searching
> trouble you, but let the veins flow,
> from the world's four corners
> life comes to me in images.

And having broached the "Canti barocchi" with less diffidence I paused at the beginning of this "Sirocco":

> And over the mountains, far above horizons
> a long strip of saffron:
> the moorish wind-swarm breaks through,
> takes the main portals by force
> the lookout-turrets on the enamel roofs,
> batters façades from the south,
> tosses scarlet hangings, blood-red pennants,
>   kites, . . .
>
> But when the wild pontifical
> folds in the west its wing of fire
> and the last red pond flakes off
> on all sides hot night rises in ambush.

It was probably, in part, the suggestion of the very bad typographical appearance of the book, but the fact is that in these lyrics I was struck by an afflatus, a rapture that made me think of the better pages of Dino Campana. The vocabulary is often recherché, but the word carries little weight: the harmony is that of a modern polytonal composer. I found myself thinking vaguely—I don't know why—of those Welsh poets—of Dylan Thomas, when he was not writing like an utter drunk—who seem to use a primordial excavated tongue, with no indulgence toward Latinisms. One cannot carry such comparisons too far; I was soon convinced of this on reading "Veneris Venefica Agrestis," a poem that is not part of the "Canti barocchi":

> She rises from low scrub, her face—
> merry, stern—bound in a black kerchief
> seems of dried chestnut, the hair escaping
> is not soft fleece but
> goat-kink; when she passes
> (upright or stooped, you can't tell) her
> gnarled brown foot
> is a root that suddenly breaks from the
> ground and walks.
>
> . . .
>
> She rules, it seems, the force
> of waxing moons
> that swells bark and alternates
> the invincible ferments
> floodtides, sap. . . .
> Pronubial as the birds
> that carry distant seeds

she brings arcane graftings.

. . .

This is no Venus, but a witch. Still a distant echo of
D'Annunzio came to me: the same kind that crops out in
some old yarn by Pea. Analogous is the proliferation of
images in catalogues, series. But how far we are here from
anything Parnassian and D'Annunzian, and how lean, in-
tense, and sharpened is the diction!

D'Annunzio is, in the recent Italian tradition, a little like
Hugo in his French posterity, from Baudelaire on down: he
is present in everyone because he experimented with or
touched upon every stylistic and prosodic possibility of our
time. In this sense to have learned nothing from him would
be a very bad sign.

I had hardly finished leafing through the little book when
Giuseppe Ravegnani, who was preparing a meeting—or
clash—between the literati of two different generations, asked
me to take part in that conference by presenting a new
writer, a young one; and I replied that I would talk about
Lucio Piccolo. Having assumed the obligation, I began to
worry, to reflect. If this poet—I said to myself—is a novice,
as everything leads me to believe, what road will he travel
from here on? His poetry is just on the brink of individuality;
suspended in antecedent fact or in post factum, it would
lose all its worth if it became the manner—and the career—
of an oneiric and surrealistic poet. Could I really wish the
unknown Piccolo "success"? Wasn't it better to let him live
and write in his distant retreat?

Two or three weeks passed and I had not moved beyond
this point in my preoccupations when the visit of Lucio Pic-

colo, in person, on his way to San Pellegrino, was announced to me. To my surprise I discovered that the young poet had been born in 1903 [1901, ed.] , which is to say barely seven years after his sponsor. Alas, what would become of the meetings between men of different generations? I found myself in the presence of Baron Lucio Piccolo di Calanovella,* a writer as yet unpublished, yes, but an accomplished musician, a student of philosophy who could read Husserl and Wittgenstein in the original, trained Greek scholar, knowledgeable in the entire field of European poetry, old and new, a reader, for example, of Gerard Manley Hopkins and of Yeats, whose esoteric inclinations he shares. In short, I was confronted by a savant so learned and well-informed that truly the idea of having to present him embarrassed me immeasurably. Lucio Piccolo has read *tous les livres* in the solitude of his estate at Capo d'Orlando, but follows no school. The foreign poet—Dylan Thomas—who had happened to come to mind was actually the only one with whom he was as yet not familiar. I know now that Piccolo has filled even this lacuna.

This, then, is the way the person I have tried to describe (at least from the point of view of his civil, "statistical," and cultural status) appeared to me: a very unusual man, a man forever in flight, resembling Carlo Emilio Gadda, a man whom the crisis of our age has hurled outside time. You will find his distant kin in picture-galleries. "An El Greco figure," Leonetta Cecchi Pieraccini said of him at their first meeting. At the San Pellegrino tournament he came and went without saying a word. I don't think he possesses oratorical abilities.

* Cousin of Giuseppe Tomasi, Prince of Lampedusa, who wrote *The Leopard.*

Great speakers existed in his family (a certain Tasca di Cutò, who belongs to the maternal side) but among the males of his line he is the only one in whom discourse has been sublimated into poetry. I would not venture to guess how much his considerable culture has profited his poetic formation. Perhaps self-criticism hindered him in the beginning, but later it surely helped him to crystallize his highly individual undertaking. In that he is truly a poet of our time. I would be tempted to attribute to him the Husserlian theme of which he spoke to us at San Pellegrino: the contradiction between a universe changing but concrete, real, and a self, absolute but unreal because it lacks tangibility, but would I not be defining thereby a current of metaphysical poetry which has always existed in various aspects? In the poems Piccolo has added to his small book, doubling its size (they are the first ten listed in the table of contents) the poet modifies, somewhat, the first impression he made upon us. Still life or the almanac moon or the Epinal image seem to have replaced the impromptu. It is improbable that these are truly the poet's most recent works. Nevertheless they permit us to fix the limits of his range: the terra-cotta crèche, surrealist objectivism ("The Conjurer") and the decorative panel ("The Hunt") in which the inventions of traditional verse and rhyme hark back curiously to the free verse in vogue around 1915-20, but against an entirely different harmonic background. In general the popular theme appears, in Piccolo, dissolved and transformed, very like the folklore motif in Bartók's music. Piccolo's most assured poetry is manifest, however, where the masks (*personae*) that populate his solitary life are set in whirling motion: in the *Canti barocchi*, that is, in those poems—like "Inconstant World," "The Bony Knuckles Try," the Leonardian "The Soul and Sleights of Hand," and others—in which the gust of the rhythm already attains full structural function, without creating, around the isolated word, zones of silence in which the world itself does not manage to persist, to echo.

The literary future of Lucio Piccolo seems wholly unpredictable: a true development of his poetry could only take place along lines of simplification, anything but easy when one has only one life to live. Surely the few lyrics of this poet will survive as the rare fruit of a poetic season which has shown itself, in these last years, as rather meager. There is no doubt that even without the error in postage to which I owe the reading of the 9 *lyrics*, in one way or another Lucio Piccolo's poetry would not have gone unnoticed. The sound of the horn that reaches us from Capo d'Orlando is not the Oliphant of a survivor, but a voice everyone can hear echoing in himself. All the rest (sources, possible developments, progeny, various difficulties of interpretation, problems which the poet does not pose to himself and which, naturally, he does not resolve) form part of a critical maze into which we have no desire to venture today. Enough for now to have the poetic thicket of Piccolo, this nature open and at the same time forbidding, freely luxuriating and yet ordered, like a puppet theatre. Cosmopolitan *gran signore* and countryman, roving fashioner of terra-cotta figures, sedentary piper who can draw unheard-of melodies even from a broken reed, Piccolo is not sure himself, perhaps, what he is giving us today and may be giving us in the future. To know him through himself, indeed at the cost of absurd misinterpretations, will be the task of his critics of tomorrow: if tomorrow there will still be critics who read the books of poets.

EUGENIO MONTALE